Winning at Flower Shows

Winning at Flower Shows

Jack Kramer

Fulcrum Publishing

Golden, Colorado

Library of Congress Cataloging-in-Publication Data
Kramer, Jack, 1927–
        Winning at flower shows / Jack Kramer
              p.   cm.
        Includes bibliographical references (p.   ) and index
        ISBN 1-55591-155-2
        1. Flower shows. 2. Plants, Ornamental—Showing.   I. Title
SB441.K73 1995
635.9'079—dc20

Printed in the United States of America
0   9   8   7   6   5   4   3   2   1

Fulcrum Publishing
350 Indiana Street, Suite 350
Golden, Colorado 80401-5093
(800) 992-2908

Contents

Acknowledgments

It is difficult to individually thank all of the people who contributed to this book—mainly because the majority of thanks goes to the many, many people who are part of various plant societies:

The Begonia Society
The Orchid Society
The Bromeliad Society
The African Violet Society
The Cactus and Succulent Society
The Geranium Society

All societies and their people responded freely to my queries and gave freely of their knowledge, and to all I say thank you.

I also wish to thank many show officials for allowing me to roam shows and ask questions. And once again I thank the thousands of plants I have grown through the years and the many orchids and bromeliads I have judged at local shows.

INTRODUCTION

Best of Show

Because of the growing ecological movement and its concern for the environment, more and more people are now aware of the importance of flora and fauna. The flower children of the 60s have become the flower-loving adults of the 90s, and attendance at flowers shows (of all kinds), with almost half a million visiting the 1993 flower show in Philadelphia, increases yearly. And the flower shows themselves are proliferating, offering everyone from eight to eighty chances to display their creative efforts with flowers.

Prize-winning flowers are stunningly beautiful, dazzling the eyes and bringing solace to the soul. But you cannot be a casual grower if you want to win the best of shows; you must invest patience, time, work and money in a specific group of plants if you want to produce specimen plants, those large and mature gems that are beautiful in all respects.

You cannot buy award-winning specimen plants; you have to grow them yourself. But raising your own showstoppers is immensely satisfying, allowing you to have some fun as well as providing great therapy in today's fast-moving world because growing plants slows you down and settles your nerves. Knowing the right tricks and following the hints we discuss here will help you grow specimen orchids, bromeliads, cacti and succulents, begonias, gesneriads and geraniums that will be more than suitable for exhibition. These are the plants I have grown throughout the years, and here I share with you the information I have attained by cultivating these floral treasures.

I have not included shows for flower arranging or for specimen garden flowers such as chrysanthemums or dahlias. That is beyond our scope here, but there are many fine books on the subjects.

After starting with a few orchids or geraniums, soon you will find yourself growing plants you think are the best, and you will want to share both your expertise and the plants' beauty with other flower lovers. Whether you grow orchids, bromeliads or gesneriads, you can enter various shows and display your personal showmanship.

Growing only one group of plants is not boring because thousands of species and varieties are in each family. For example, orchids alone contain thirty-five thousand wild species and thousands more hybrids. Within each group are so many plant families that one will attract you. Years ago, I entered my orchids and bromeliads in various flower shows in San Francisco; the experiences were great fun and very exciting. Eventually, I judged a number of plant shows. But when I began a series of lectures to garden clubs and plant societies, I became aware that few people knew of the wide, wide world of flower/plant shows or how and where to exhibit their plants. This book will help all plant hobbyists who want to try your hands at plant exhibiting, the ultimate reward of growing plants.

—Jack Kramer

SECTION ONE

GROWING YOUR OWN

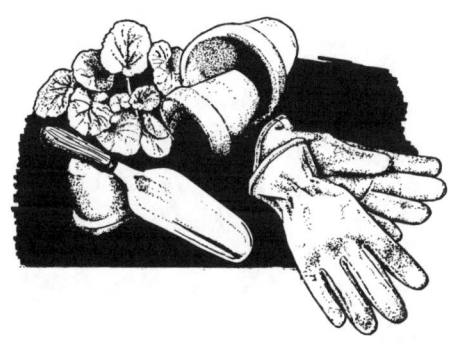

CHAPTER ONE

Selecting a Specialty

WHAT YOU GROW DEPENDS UPON your unique and personal tastes in flowers, form, color and ease of culture. I am recommending the following groups of plants because I have actually grown them all. You may find you like the stunning flowers of the orchids or the resilient and odd beauty of the bromeliads. Cacti and succulents offer a somewhat surrealistic attractiveness; their toughness ensures easier culture than with other flowering plants.

The gesneriads, including the African violets, are beautiful and come in many varieties, but I have always had just limited success with them. On the other hand, some fans of the violets find them fairly easy to raise.

Each family of plants has its own unique season of bloom; for example, most begonias bloom in the summer, but the rhizomatous kinds come into flower mainly in the winter. Trying to force plants into bloom or to delay blooming involves patience, endurance and work. And some plants bloom during the day, while others put forth their blossoms at night, which means that some plants, such as certain orchids, bloom when days are short, whereas other orchids bloom when days are long.

If you are growing just one group of plants, you will find it fairly easy to determine which varieties (species) bloom when; this information is quite important when you are trying to get plants ready to show at a specific date. Following the discussion of each plant is a listing of bloom times.

BEGONIAS

There are numerous groups within this plant family; the main groups are the angel-wing, semperflorens, tuberous rooted, Rex, hirsute and rhizomatous begonias. The angel-wings usually flower in the winter, but if you expose them to artificial light to lengthen the days in October for eight weeks, you can delay flowering until the spring. The semperflorens will produce more flowers in their spring season if they are grown under high-intensity light for twelve hours a day. Tuberous rooted begonias are long-day plants that normally bloom in the summer. You can prolong the bloom period by growing these begonias under artificial light. Rex begonias require more humidity and shade than other begonias, but some species can be grown indoors successfully. They will produce more leaves later in their normal season if you lengthen the days. The hirsutes and rhizomatous begonias are the easiest types to grow; they do not mind adverse conditions, and several of them tolerate less humidity than other begonias do.

Limiting your indoor begonias to only one group enables you to show and enter only one category in your specialty. Also, growing just one group simplifies caring for the plants because they will all require the same cultural conditions. All begonias require time, effort and genuine interest for successful cultivation. But some are easier to grow than others, and some are more dependable regarding bloom.

Begonias are mainly from Brazil, Mexico and Africa. Some thrive in bright sun, others in bright light and others in semishade. Although begonias are often considered shade plants, they actually want some sunshine, especially in the winter. In summer, begonias need some protection from the noonday sun.

Begonias adjust to varying temperatures; average home conditions of 72° to 80°F during the day and 60° to 68°F at night throughout the winter are fine. I generally recommend growing plants in terra-cotta pots, but decorative containers are especially nice for begonias. You can plant your begonias in the standard clay pot and then place the pot inside a larger decorative container. Most decorative containers do not have drainage holes, so you should follow certain precautions when planting directly in them. First, lay a layer of lava stone as a drainage bed, interspersed with some charcoal chunks to keep the soil sweet. Elevate the container above the floor or table on a wood, metal or cork mat.

An unglazed decorative container is the best because it is porous, allowing moisture to evaporate slowly through its walls. Glazed containers, although they prevent water evaporation, are very attractive and available in all kinds of shapes.

Overwatering can kill begonias. Let plants dry out before watering again so roots have time to absorb all moisture. Indoors, begonias need feeding because repeated watering washes out nutrients. Fertilizer will produce healthy begonias with strong leaf color and fine blooms. I use a 10-10-5 soluble fertilizer, applying only half the amount recommended on the package label.

Fertilize plants when they are actively growing, usually in the spring and summer. In cold weather, some begonias are dormant, so feed these plants only about every six weeks. Give plants Atlas Fish Emulsion once every two weeks in the summer, not at all during the rest of the year. Each month, strongly spray your begonias with water to leach out chemicals that have accumulated in the soil. Never feed freshly potted begonias because the new soil has enough nutrients to sustain the plants for some time. And never feed sick plants. Finally, never apply food to the leaves with a spray; the Rex and hirsute types of begonias especially resent lingering moisture on their leaves.

Bloom Times for Begonias

Spring
Angel-wings
B. 'Lady Clare'
B. 'Limminghei'
B. 'Lucerne'
B. 'Leo C. Shippy'

Summer
Trailing begonias
B. 'Orange Rubra'
B. ricinifolia
B. Coccinea alzasco

Autumn
B. 'Beatrice Haddrell'
B. 'Credneri'
B. 'Drosti'
B. 'Mrs. Fred D. Scripps'

Winter
B. 'Bessie Buxton'
Erythrophylla
B. 'Maphil'

BROMELIADS

Painted feather, queen's tears, rainbow plant, flaming sword, painted fingernail, black chantini—these are only a few of the many glamorous popular names given to the superlative bromeliads. Almost indestructible, these plants are excellent for indoor decoration because they adjust to home conditions and require less care than most other plants. Easy to grow, bromeliads are available in different sizes, from miniatures to giants; most are just the right size for indoor growing. Bromeliads' foliage is highly colorful, the flower scapes are beautiful and the berries of many species last three to four months. Bromeliads are also ideal for outdoor culture where temperatures do not drop below freezing.

Bromeliads have become very popular and gain new fans daily. The varied family offers flowers, unusual foliage and easy maintenance. Many local shows are devoted to bromeliads (the societies and guilds can provide local show dates).

Aechmea is the most popular genus. *A. fasciata* is a long-day plant that can be induced to bloom in winter, if necessary, by lengthening the days with artificial light for ten hours each day for at least one month.

Billbergias are other favorite bromeliads; they normally bloom in the spring or summer. They can be induced to earlier blooming by applying artificial light from October to February for eight hours a day for eight weeks.

Most Bromeliads are from South America, with the greatest number from Brazil. Many are also found in Mexico and Central America, and a few are found within the United States. In nature, bromeliads are mainly epiphytes (air lovers), growing high in treetops in partial sunlight and using tree branches as anchors. Most epiphytes have thick leaves. Contrary to what some people think, bromeliads are *not* parasites.

Some species of bromeliads grow in the ground in shade; these plants are called *terrestrials* and have thick and spiny leaves. Still other species grow on rocks, and some grow in full sun in the desert. Many genera grow under all three conditions. Some even live on other plants, and a few bromeliads use telephone wires or poles as footholds.

Any kind of bromeliad is almost always found in areas of good air circulation because air is vital to the plants' growth. Some of these plants have a vase- or bowl-shaped formation of leaves, which acts as a receptacle for food and holds as much as a full cup of water. In the jungle, organic matter, including insects, small frogs and lizards, drops into the receptacle. Some of these creatures die within the receptacle, furnishing the plants with necessary nutrients. But in cultivation, bromeliads are pest-free; their tough foliage is almost immune to insects (and pets).

When growing naturally, many bromeliads do not have an extensive root system. As long as their receptacles hold water, the plants can survive a long time without additional moisture. In cultivation, attached to driftwood or grouped in dish gardens, bromeliads last quite dry for many weeks. However, if grown in containers in a porous soil mixture, the plants develop larger root systems, which in turn require additional moisture.

Aechmeas have a circular rosette of thick leaves; Nidulariums have flattened tops that look like pressed fans.

Vertical and tubular growth is prevalent among Billbergias. Large Tillandsias have narrow, tapered leaves arranged in a graceful palm effect; smaller species have a tentacle or bristling growth habit. The foliage of the Vrieseas is rosette or tapered (these plants resemble handsome small bushes). Dyckias look like cactus, and Cryptanthus species resemble starfish. Pitcairnias have spindly vertical foliage and attractive flowers; many Quesnelias have rosette or tubular growth patterns.

Bromeliad flowers are red, pink, lavender or blue, although white, yellow and green flowers also abound. Two or three species of Tillandsias and one Aechmea species have flowers with a sweet fragrance, but most bromeliad flowers are scentless.

Bromeliads' bracts and spikes are vividly colored for a long time in many species. The forms of the spikes range from the branched candelabra growth of the Aechmeas to the flamboyant and pendant sprays of the Billbergias or the low flowers crowns in the center of various Neoregelias. Some Guzmanias have a star-shaped inflorescence. And small Orthophytums look like tiny fountains of spiny leaves crowned red when in bloom.

But even without flowers, bromeliads are still most attractive because of their foliage, which comes with varied markings and in assorted colors. The foliage of some of these plants is green-gray to yellow to red to brown. The Aechmeas have beautiful plum- and wine-colored leaves. Some species have mottled foliage, some sport horizontal or vertical stripes, a few have spotted leaves and the leaves of still other bromeliads are magnificently variegated. I find the frosted green coloring of certain Billbergias the most handsome among the bromeliads. As houseplants, bromeliads are different and a pleasing contrast to other indoor plants.

I grow about forty plants at a time, ten for each season, which provides me with year-round color even if some of the plants do fail to bloom. I have had only two bromeliads that were total losses for me, and it was my fault both times. I potted one plant too tightly—since the drainage was poor, the crown rotted. I put the other bromeliad on an open porch where wind knocked it down and severely bruised it.

I keep the natural "vases" of my bromeliads filled with water throughout spring, summer and fall, flushing out the waste and refilling every week. In winter, I let the plants dry out somewhat. Throughout the year, I let plants dry out between waterings. During the summer and fall, I water plants about every third day; in the winter and spring, I water every fourth or fifth day.

Pot epiphytic and rock-growing bromeliads in fir bark; this material dries quickly and provides excellent drainage, which is vital to the plants' growth. Orchid bark is also a suitable growing medium for these species. Terrestrial-type bromeliads need a mixture of leaf mold, manure, sand and some crushed rock.

Bromeliads' leaves are hard and durable; their core is their weakest part. If the plant's receptacles hold water too long and the water does not drain off naturally in the growing medium, the plant's core may rot. Do not pot bromeliads too tightly or water will not be able to drain off and rot will develop.

Most bromeliad species do best grown in small containers. Small containers dry out faster than larger ones, thus precluding a stagnant compost. The standard orchid terra-cotta pot, 4 to 5 inches in diameter, is fine, even for larger bromeliads. I grow a *Billbergia zebrina* that is almost 4 feet tall in a 4-inch pot. The plant is top-heavy, especially when its receptacle is filled with water, so I prop it up against slender bamboo stakes pushed deep into the growing medium at the edge of the pot. I loop string around the stakes to hold them together.

Bloom Times for Bromeliads

Spring
Aechmea chantinii
A. fulgens
A. orlandiana
Billbergia pyramidalis
Guzmania magnifica
G. musaca
Tillandsia (many)

Summer
Aechmea leuddemanniana
A. maginali
A. ramosa
Billbergia amoena
B. nutans
B. pyramidalis
B. zebrina
Guzmania monostachia
G. vittata
Vriesea carinata
V. fenestralis

Autumn
Aechmea mertensii
A. mooreana
Billbergia elegans
B. nutans
B. venezuelana
Neoregelia carolinae
N. marmorata
Nidularium innocentii
Quesnalis arvensis
Vriesea carinata

Winter
Aechmea racinae
A. ramosa
A. recurvata
Billbergia 'Fantasia'
B. leitzei
Guzmania magnifica
Neoregelia 'Painted Lady'
Tillandsia streptophylla
Vriesea scwackeana

CACTI AND SUCCULENTS

Cacti are beautiful and, in some instances, bizarre plants, and hobbyists throughout the country have outstanding collections. At flower shows, cacti are prime attractions. Cacti can be attractive indoor plants providing dramatic accent.

The varieties of cacti are almost limitless. Some cacti are shaped like candelabras; others are formed like giant columns. Other cacti look like globes or barrels. These different shapes provide a source for interest in all interior areas. For example, the large candelabra- or column-type cacti, such as Cleistocactus and Trichocereus, boldly highlight corners. The barrel- or globe-shaped cacti, such as Mammillaria or Lobivia, provide desirable mass in a room.

Plant colors are as varied as the shapes: gold, leather green, apple green, with shades and hues in between, offer an infinite array of green and gold tones to complement interiors. Cacti also come in various sizes: small plants that make beautiful dish gardens displayed on tables, medium-sized varieties that accent window gardens and large cacti that supply a keynote in the living room. And if you love flowers, Christmas cacti, Epiphyllums and Rhipsalis are ideal for hanging baskets, where they display a cascade of color. The flowering cacti are quite distinct from their desert cousins because they grow naturally in moist and shady jungles.

With few exceptions, cacti are leafless plants with flattened or ribbed bodies. The stems, rather than leaves as in most other plants, manufacture food. Most cacti have spines, but not all spines are needlelike; many species bear furry spines that are as soft as velvet. Other cacti, such as *Cephalocereus senilis* (old man cactus), are covered with silky hairs that protect the outside of the plants from the drying wind and sun.

Most cacti are succulent plants, but not all succulents are cacti. Succulent plants appear in many plant families, such as the lily. The term "succulent" is applied to plants that have developed water-storage cells in their leaves. Succulent cacti are either epiphytic or desert types. The epiphytes grow in trees in the jungle and have flattened leaflike stems, such as the Christmas cactus and Rhipsalis. Desert cacti are variable in form; they are columnar- or globe-shaped, large or small. Some cacti have pronounced ribs so the plants can expand and contract as they gain water; other cacti have tubercles.

The following plants are succulents, not cacti; I am including them because so many of them, such as the Euphorbias, resemble cacti. Also, some of the succulents are such superb indoor plants that they are worth including. For example, agaves and aloes can be beautiful in a home and potential award-winning plants.

Many Euphorbias resemble cacti. They generally are columnar or tree types and provide dramatic highlights and will last several years without attention. Euphorbias need bright, but not necessarily sunny, locations. Grow plants in well-drained soil kept moderately moist year-round except in the winter when they should be rested dry for about six weeks. Euphorbias tolerate low humidity and a wide range of temperatures.

This fascinating group of plants includes my favorite, the century plant, which I had for ten years, until my cat one day discovered the milky juice within the leaves; in time, he finally killed the plant. The group also includes some of the Amaryllis family, with its incredible foliage color, from gray-green to dark green to slate gray. Agaves thus provide unique color indoors, making them superb for decorative effect. The plants have a rosette-style growth, and most are armed with spines on the edges of their leaves.

Agaves must be grown in large containers and in sandy soil to look their best. Give the plants bright light.

Aloes are often confused with agaves because they look somewhat like them. Native to Africa and Madagascar and members of the lily family, aloes have unusual flowers. Not all aloes are decorative plants; some become too straggly indoors, but the rosette-type aloes have a uniform growth that is desirable.

Grow aloes in rich soil. Plants need more sun than the agaves. Aloes need lots of water in the summer to prosper.

The leafy yuccas are becoming more and more popular as houseplants. They do not resemble cacti as much as the other plants mentioned within this section, but they do have dense rosettes of sword-shaped leaves and provide excellent color indoors. Yuccas need a rich soil and a bright location. They are not sensitive regarding temperatures, and they grow almost untended. For the most effective interior decoration, use yuccas in ornamental, tapered containers.

The very-easy-to-grow Haworthias are usually small plants. Most are spiny and look like cacti. They tolerate shade and are excellent houseplants. The leaves are usually in rosettes, but the stems sometimes become elongated. Haworthias like a rather cool temperature (60°F) and a sandy soil; they need scant watering. They are especially effective for dish gardens.

From the dry regions of Africa and the East Indies, Stapelias are bizarre but beautiful succulents, small and branched at their bases. The large flowers are incredibly complex and bloom well indoors. The plants need warmth during the day but coolness at night; give them some shade in the summer. Grow stapelias in a rich soil.

Bloom Times for Cacti

Spring	Summer
Echinocactus	Echinopsis
Echinocereus	Mammillaria

Autumn
Notocactus
Rebutia

Winter
Rebutia
Parodia

GERANIUMS
(Pelargoniums)

Geraniums have been favorite plants since Queen Victoria's day, and as long ago as 1750, the plants were flourishing here in America. But today's geraniums are far removed from those of yesteryear because of hybridization, which has added multitudes of new forms.

Pelargoniums (the official name of geraniums) are from South America. These shrublike or climbing plants have large round-headed clusters of beautiful flowers. The geraniums are generally classified into these groups: (1) Martha Washington (*P. domesticum*), (2) house geranium (*P. hortorum*) (also called zonal [*P. pelatatum*]), and (3) ivy-leaved and scented-leaved. Sometimes species and fancy-leaved categories are added to the classifications. Finally, dwarf types of geraniums are also available.

Geraniums offer almost constant color when grown cool at night (about 60°F), and they must have at least four hours of good sun during the day. In the appropriate outdoor conditions, some geraniums will even grow into small trees.

Indoors, geraniums must be grown in a standard houseplant soil that contains a bit of acidity. Water plants freely, and then let them dry out before the next watering. Because the plants bloom best when potbound, grow them in small terra-cotta containers.

Give the ivy-leaved and Martha Washington types a slight rest in winter; water only enough to keep the soil barely moist.

Do not overwater geraniums. Avoid high humidity, and to prevent rot, do not mist the foliage. Feed plants when they are actively growing. I use a 20-20-20 plant food, but the foods made specifically for geraniums are fine also.

Zonals are the geraniums we are most familiar with and the most apt to win at flower shows. They have scalloped leaves and brilliantly colored single and double flowers. Plants grow to about 30 inches or more, but there are so many subgroups of zonals that it is difficult to give average height or growth measurements.

Zonals need plenty of sun and a free flow of air. Humidity can ruin these geraniums, and they do not like to be crowded. The plants, which bloom mainly in the summer, need good feeding. I apply my 20-20-20 plant food twice a month during the warm months, not at all during the rest of the year.

These regal plants spout bowers of stunning flowers in the spring; the flowers are white, tinged with lavender, red or purple. Some of the varieties display pansy-type flowers.

The Lady Washington geraniums grow lavishly with cool nights (60°F) and plenty of sun during the day. Grow them directly in the outdoor garden, or cultivate them in pots on patios and terraces. These geraniums need a rather fertile soil—a good African violet soil is fine. Let plants dry out between waterings; feed them with 20-20-20 food every two weeks during the growing season but not at all the rest of the year when the plants take a slight rest.

Windowsill garden favorites for years, these geraniums are valued for their nutmeg, lemon (*P. crispum*), eucalyptus, peppermint (*P. tomentosum*), rose (*P. graveolens*), apple and numerous other scents. Plants grow to medium height but are somewhat rangy in appearance. Leaf structure varies from deeply scalloped to maple-leaved types to very small leaves in the lemon-scented varieties. The small flowers are in clusters.

Scented geraniums thrive on sun and grow lushly in pots. These plants are especially prized at flower shows and always win many awards.

The ivy-leaved geraniums (*P. pelatatum*) are quite welcome at flower shows because they brim with stunning and vibrant color (many display white and purple flowers). These plants are particularly attractive in baskets and can be grown indoors or outdoors.

With plenty of sun, the ivy-leaved geraniums will bloom throughout the winter months. They must be grown with nighttime temperatures below 68°F; they will even thrive at 55°F. Keep the soil barely moist during the winter, and feed them only about once a month. Pinch back plants to encourage flower bud formation for good display.

Bloom Times for Geraniums

Spring
Zonals
Martha Washington

Summer
Martha Washington
Many zonals

Autumn
Scented-leaved

Winter
Ivy-leaved

GESNERIADS

African violets (Saintpaulias) are the most popular members of this large group of attractive plants. In recent years, other gesneriads such as the Smithianthas, Rechsteinerias, Episcias, Kohlerias, Columneas and Streptocarpus have become popular as houseplants; unfortunately, many species in the family are becoming extinct.

Gesneriads grow easily with minimum care, needing only a shady location, even moisture and routine feeding. Even though gesneriads are tropical plants, they do not need humid, hot conditions; they prosper at about 78°F during the day and 68°F at night. However, their tropical heritage does dictate that gesneriads receive light shading because, in their native habitat, most of these plants grow as terrestrials on the floors of forests where the light is subdued. Most gesneriads die down after flowering, such as the Gloxinias, but even those that grow all year, such as the Episcias and African violets, need a brief resting period with minimum water a few months of the year (usually in winter).

The foliage generally is hairy-leaved, in many cases velvety. Flowers range from 4 to 5 inches (Streptocarpus) to 1 inch in diameter (Hypocyrtas). Bright colors are the main gesneriad characteristic; some Episcias are especially vibrant. Plants can be 2-inch miniatures (Streptocarpus) or 26-inch high standards (Kohlerias). Some Columnea and Episcia varieties are pendulous.

In the winter, plants need supplementary lighting to produce their best flower crop. Keep grow-type lighting tubes on eighteen hours a day in the winter; the additional lighting will also produce more compact growth. Streptocarpus, Achimenes, Kohlerias and some other gesneriads may bloom somewhat later in the normal summer season, which can be beneficial if shows are held in the fall.

Most lipstick vines (Aeschynanthus) are trailing epiphytes, to 3 feet long, with dark and glossy green leaves and red or orange flowers. The plants prefer a partially shady but still light location and evenly moist soil at all times. Fertilize with 10-20-10 food during plants' growth periods to produce flowers. After plants bloom, curtail watering.

Either trailing plants or upright growers to 3 feet tall, Columneas display decorative buttonlike or elliptical leaves. Flowers are usually orange, but varieties with yellow flowers are now available. Because Columneas are basically epiphytic, plant them in a rather loose mix of equal parts of small-grade fir bark and soil. Keep the growing medium evenly moist; fertilize with 10-20-10 food every third week. Give Columneas sun in the winter and a partially shady location in the summer.

These 14- to 20-inch long exotic epiphytes are called peacock plants because their leaves are so colorful and the summer-produced small, funnel-shaped flowers are brilliant red, white or other colors. Most Episcias are trailers and need copious watering and bright light but not sun. In decent growing conditions, the plants can grow throughout the winter without going dormant. Grow Episcias in temperatures never lower than 60°F at night, and fertilize them with 10-20-10 food every third week during growth but not at all in the winter.

African violets need bright light in the spring and summer and a little sun the rest of the year. Keep the soil evenly moist, and be sure drainage is good because stagnant water will kill the plants. Nighttime temperature should never be below 60°F; fertilize plants one a week with African violet food. There are dozens of flower shows to exibit your violets.

Endless varieties, from miniatures and dwarfs to standardized plants, make up this popular group. The small plants have velvety or smooth, scalloped or wavy, heart-shaped or elliptical, green or variegated foliage. The flowers, in mostly shades of blue, lavender, pink or white, come in many forms, including single, double, frilled and semidouble.

Gloxinias are glamorous plants from tropical Brazil and sport single or double tubular- or slipper-shaped flowers in vivid colors. Hybrids bloom at various times throughout the year. Gloxinias prefer coolness and shade, the cooler and shadier, the better. When flowers begin fading, reduce watering, remove the tops of the plants and store the bulbs in a cool and shady location. Keep the soil barely moist, and let the bulbs rest about eight weeks. Then repot bulbs in fresh soil in a larger pot (one bulb to a pot). To repot, place the bulb with its hollow side up in the pot and cover the bulb with soil. Keep the soil evenly moist; the room temperature should be about 60°F. Increase water and warmth when growth starts to flourish.

Streptocarpus blooms on and off for many months with white, pink, rose, salmon or blue flowers. Plants need bright light and evenly moist soil. Feed cape primrose twice a month when plants are actively growing, but when plants rest, stop feeding, and water only to prevent plants from wilting. When fresh growth begins, repot plants in new soil.

Hypocyrta's small orange flowers look like tiny goldfish. This gesneriad produces masses of handsome dark green leaves. Kohlerias have colorful and attractive flowers. Most of these gesneriads are trailers, but some species grow upright.

Rechsteinerias, from the South American rain forest, bloom with red, pink or orange flowers in the summer. The leaves are velvety. The red or orange flowers of Smithiantha look like temple bells and appear from November through May. These are excellent plants to win awards because not too many people grow them.

Bloom Times for Gesneriads

Spring
Achimenes (many varieties)
Aeschynanthus
Kohleria

Summer
Episcia cupreata
E. anjou
Columnea (many hybrids)
Hypocryta strigillosa
H. nummularia

Autumn
Smithiantha cinnabarina
Rechsteineria cardinalis

Winter
Streptocarpus (many)
Saintpaulia (African violet) blooms at all seasons of the year, depending on the specific variety. Check your mail-order supplier.

ORCHIDS

Orchids are the flowers of the four seasons because there are species for spring, summer, autumn and winter. You can grow as few as six orchids and still have bloom almost year-round. The dreary winter months can be brightened with the flowers of the Mormodes, Miltonias, Odontoglossums, Oncidiums, Cycnoches and Coelogynes among others. In spring, the amazing Dendrobiums, Calanthes and Apasias display their blooms; the Brassias, Brassavolas and Epidendrums blossom in the summer. In addition, the thousands of miniature orchids are delightful to grow.

To successfully cultivate orchids, you should be familiar with the nature of the species you are raising. The natural flowering time of the species will also affect your success. Sometimes orchids imported from a part of the world with seasons opposite ours, as in South America, arrive in our winter with a flower spike already visible; in the United States, that same plant would not be ready for flowering until the spring.

Different orchid species have different bloom characteristics. Many of the botanicals are spray orchids, with fifty or a hundred tiny flowers opening on a branch at one time. Some orchids bloom in clusters; others produce single flowers. Most orchids, such as *Cattleya forbesii* and *Lycaste aromatica*, bloom only once a year, but some species, like *Miltonia roezlii* and *Coelogyne massangeana*, will bloom more than once within a year if grown well. And some orchids, such as *Epidendrum o'brienianum* and *Brassavola nodosa*, are in flower almost all year. Some orchids will produce only one or two flowers the first year you grow them, but once they are established in your conditions, they will become stronger and produce four or five flowers. Finally, if you supply high-intensity light for some species, you will have more flowers during December than during January and February.

Orchids prefer short or long days regarding blooming. For example, Phalaenopsis generally require short days to bloom. If days are too long, shorten the day length by covering the windows with black cloth. Dropping the temperature slightly will also help induce budding. Vandas bloom best with short days and high temperatures. Oncidiums generally are long-day plants; you may have to provide additional artificial light to induce blooming. Cymbidiums like long days and cool nights.

In the winter, most orchids will thrive in average home temperatures of 56° to 63°F at night, 62° to 80°F during the day. Cool-growing genera of Odontoglossum and Miltonia need temperatures 6° to 10° cooler; warm-growing genera such as some Oncidiums and Dendrobiums need temperatures 6° to 10° warmer. However, many orchids are adaptable; when you are comfortable, so are most of your orchids. Coal, gas or radiant baseboard heating will not harm orchids.

During the hot summer months, if you do not have air-conditioning, try to keep the humidity high during very warm days. A few 90° to 100° days will not kill the orchids. Because most orchids are epiphytic, circulation of air is the most important cultural factor. I run two small fans at low speeds (directing the air away from the plants) in hot weather to keep air gently moving in the growing area. I run one fan during the winter. At night, I shut the fans off in hot weather and in winter unless the atmosphere in the growing area seems stuffy.

Orchids respond poorly to sudden changes in temperature and to drafts. When you open windows to ventilate the growing area, freshen the atmosphere indirectly by opening windows other than those right by the plants. Orchids will need more watering the more the indoor heat fluctuates in the winter because artificial heat dries out the air.

You can plant most orchids in the slotted clay pots made for commercial orchid growers. However, you can use the standard terra-cotta pot if you enlarge its drainage hole by gently hammering it out. Genus determines pot size: Dendrobiums, Lycastes and Miltonias, because of their compact pseudobulbs, do best in 4- or 5-inch-diameter pots. Laelias, Oncidiums and Cattleyas need large pots unless they are dwarf species.

To plant an orchid, fill the pot one-half to one-third its depth with broken pieces (shards) of a pot. Set the orchid in place and fill in with fresh fir bark (some growers recommend soaking the bark overnight, but I have found dry bark satisfactory); occasionally press down the bark with a blunt-edged potting stick or a piece of wood. Always work from the sides of the pot to the center until you have filled up the pot to within one inch of its rim. If necessary, stake the orchid with wire or wooden sticks; label the orchid. Most orchids require tight potting; a few do better when loosely planted.

When planting with fir bark, good drainage is essential to healthy growth; excess moisture at the root ball can kill an orchid. More orchids are killed by overwatering than any other cultural error, but this will not happen to your orchids if you plant them correctly.

After potting (or repotting) orchids, keep them in a 60° to 78°F area and out of direct sun. *Do not water plants* for at least seven to ten days, preferably two to three weeks. During that time, daily spray the immediate area around the plants with a very fine mist of water (you can also mist the pot and the very edge of the surface of the fir bark). Never spray water directly on the foliage or the bulb of a freshly potted orchid.

Fir bark lacks sufficient nitrogen, so you should fertilizer to supplement the feeding. At a nursery or florist, buy a 20-10-10 or 10-5-5 formula (figures indicate percentages of nitrogen, phosphoric acid and potash, respectively). When orchids are in active growth, feed them about every ten to fourteen days (active growth season varies by species).

Fertilize carefully because most orchid species react adversely to heavy feeding. Too much nitrogen can deter flowering. You may want to experiment with different brands of fertilizers. I find that a weak application of Atlas Fish Emulsion once a month (even in the winter) benefits my orchids.

Bloom Times for Orchids

Spring
Ascocentrum ampullaceum
Aerides odoratum
Brassavola nodosa
B. glauca
Cattleya (many)
Lycaste aromatica
L. skinneri
Dendrobium chrysotoxum
D. dalhousianum

Summer
Aerides fieldingii
Coelogyne massangena
Epidendrum ciliare
E. mariae
Oncidium leuchochilum
O. splendidum
Laelia tenebrosa

Autumn
Laelia anceps
L. gouldiana
Masdevallia coccinea
Odontoglossum citrosum
O. ure-skinneri

Winter
Cattleya (many varieties)
Phalaenopsis hybrids
(many)
Rhyncostylis gigantea
Vanda (many varieties)
Zygopetalum mackayii

CHAPTER TWO

A Winning Possibility

JUDGES HAVE FAVORED CERTAIN PLANTS FOR years. And after more than twenty years of growing, writing about and exhibiting houseplants, I feel I can offer tips that will give you a slight advantage over your competition. However, you cannot just enter any variety I discuss and expect to win a prize; you still must have a well-groomed and properly grown plant in the correct proportions and displayed in the correct container to take home the award.

BEGONIAS

Begonias comprise such a very diverse group, with some quite showy but others rather dull in comparison, that it is important to select carefully if you want to win. The fabulous hanging or tuberous trailing begonias are always show stoppers, but there is intense competition within this group.

I always preferred to enter the angel-wing begonia category; I was successful because these plants have both handsome foliage and flowers. *Begonia coccinea*, with its bright green leaves and red flowers, always gets the judges' attention, and B. 'Di Erna' wins points for its great coral flowers. Judges also like B. 'Arengtea Guttata'; B. 'Grey Feather', with fine arrow-shaped leaves and pretty white flowers and B. 'Pink Spot Lucerne'. If you are cultivating angel-wings, aim for compact growth. These plants tend to be leggy; I cut back mine early on to encourage a well-shaped plant.

The rhizomatous begonias, with gnarled rhizomes skirting the soil, can be handsome if well grown. Their varied leaf texture and shape, and the fact that some of them can reach giant proportions, make them ideal specimen plants for showing. Begonia 'Beatrice Haddrell', with exquisite leaves and pink flowers, is a long-time favorite, and a fine specimen of *B. crestabruchii* always gets the judges' eyes: these are spectacular plants when well grown. I also favor *B. erythrophlyla*, the beefsteak begonia, for its foliage. A compact *B. imperialis* 'Otto Forster', with bouquets of leaves, garners much attention at shows. And do not overlook B. 'Cleopatra' or some of its varieties because this plant is a halo of color when well cultivated and wins many awards at shows.

The hirsute begonias also receive their share of attention; these big furry-leaved plants make even beginners look good. Most species are winter-blooming. Begonia 'Alleryi' is perhaps the most popular, with frosted green leaves and white flowers, and a good candidate for flower shows. Pinch out this plant when it is growing to ensure rounded growth. Begonia 'Loma Alto' is another good choice for showing, with attention-getting plush red leaves. *Begonia venosa*, seldom shown, is also a prize winner if it is grown properly into a specimen plant, Begonia 'Mrs. Fred D. Scripps' is an old favorite whose mass of white flowers and handsome foliage always wins points. Here is a list of other good begonias for shows.

Angel-Wings

B. 'Alzasco'—brilliant red flowers

Rhizomatous

B. 'Bessie Buxton'— clusters of pink flowers

B. 'Maphil'—multicolored foliage

Hirsute

B. 'Alto Scharff'—lovely white and pink flowers edged
    red

B. metallica—handsome foliage and pink flowers

Fibrous

B. 'Corbeille de Feu'—waxy green leaves and red
    flowers

B. schmidtiana—pale pink flowers

B. serratipela—pink flowers

Basket Types

B. 'Corallina de Lucerna'—a favorite show plant

B. 'Elsie M. Frey'—delightful pink flowers

B. 'Orange Rubra'—clusters of fine orange flowers

B. 'Pink Camellia'—floriferous, pink flowers

B. 'President Carnot'—always a show stopper

B. 'Shippy's Garland'—cascades of pink flowers

Tuberous Begonias

The tuberous begonias, resplendent with their summer
show of color with cascades of flowers are really outdoor
plants but I include them here because I have grown so many
and seen them at so many flower shows. There are pendent

and upright kinds, single and double forms, camellia and picotee forms and the list goes on and on.

Certainly, if you feel you want to enter your tuberous begonia in a show, do so but be aware the competition is staggering and the placement of your plant in the proper category can be difficult to determine. It is the pendent types of begonias, of which there are many varieties, that steal the show at any exhibit.

BROMELIADS

The bromeliads have uprooted the philodendrons as carefree houseplants. The judges dote on *Aechmea fasciata*, with silver-frosted leaves and pink and blue flowers, and its improved varieties. *A. chantinii*, a large branching bromeliad with flowers that have exquisite cerise crowns, is another winner.

The Billbergias offer only a few good selections. I like *B. pyramidalis* and have always been partial to B. 'Muriel Waterman'. *B. venezuelana*, with its magnificently colored foliage, and *B. zebrina* are other notable performers at shows.

Today there are hosts of Guzmanias with really vibrantly colored flowerheads. *G. magnifica* displays a star-shaped red flowerhead. *G. sanguinea* catches the eye with its yellow and orange center crown. *G. lingulata* has star-shaped growth and an orange flower head. Its red, white and black flower- heads make *G. monostachia* very attractive. G. 'Minnie Exodus' and G. 'Symphonie' are two other excellent Guzmanias for show.

Neoregelia, the rosette-type bromeliad, is a favorite (and crowded) category at flower shows. There are so many spectacular Neoregelias that it is difficult to single out the best for exhibition. I had some luck with *N. marmorata*, which has apple-green and yellow foliage. N. 'Purple Passion' and *N. spectabilis* (dark green foliage tipped with red) are also superb.

The Nidulariums are not grown as much as the Neoregelias, but they do offer several outstanding specimens. *N. innocentii lineatum* is dramatic, with variegated leaves and a deep purple center. *N. innocentii tricolor* also evokes comment because of its spectacular foliage. And if you have the rare *Orthophytum navoides*, by all means, exhibit it because its red rosettes are quite captivating.

Tillandsia, a favorite bromeliad genus, has many plants, but only a few are award winning because they tend to be leggy and spindly. Also, because there are so many Tillandsias, identification in this group is extremely difficult.

There are numerous Vrieseas that are potential winners. *V. reginae* is quite handsome, with tall spikes of color; *V. splendens* 'Meyers Favorite' and V. 'Rubin' are other good show candidates. Here are other bromeliad choices for flower shows.

Aechmea

A. leudemanniana—red bracts and blue petals

A. orlandiana—mottled and colored foliage with
    ivory flowers

A. racinae—fine red pendant flowers

A. recurvata v. ortegesii—low pink flowerhead

Billbergia

B. 'Fantasia'—scarlet pendant bracts and pink-blue
    flowers

B. leptopoda—pink bracts, green and blue flowers

B. pyramidalis v. concolor—dense pink and red
    flowerhead

Guzmania

G. lingulata 'Peacocki'—flowers have fiery orange
    center

Neoregelia

N. carolinae v. tricolor—lovely variegated foliage

Quesnelia

Q. arvensis—handsome red flower crowns

Tillandsia

T. anceps—arching leaves, pale green or rose bracts

T. caput medusae—vivid blue flowers

T. cyanea—large fans of purple flowers

T. juncea—red flower crown

T. streptophylla—unusual growth habit

T. tricolor—pink and red flowers

Vriesea

V. carinata—sword-shaped red-and-yellow
    flowerhead

V. carinata 'Mariae'—the painted feather plant

V. fenestralis—stunning foliage

V. imperialis—red and yellow flowers

V. petropolitana—orange and yellow flowers

CACTI AND SUCCULENTS

I have a friend in California who always wins the most ribbons for his cacti and succulents. He concentrates on succulents and has won great favor with *Agave huachensis*, which is exceedingly beautiful, looking like a granite sculpture. The very popular *A. victoriae reginae* also curries favor with judges. This plant is a ball of green color with white margins.

My friend is also a master at growing Echeverias. Some of the large Echeverias, with their pink-pearl leaves, are outstanding; there are many new hybrids within this group. *Euphorbia obesa*, the basketball plant, is odd, but because few people grow it, it is a good plant to enter: its multicolored basketball-type growth always attracts attention.

For me, the Haworthias have never been showy; most of mine have been small. The endangered Dudleyas have attractive white powdery leaves. The Stapelias and Hoodias, with massive star-shaped flowers, have never attracted me, yet they always seem to come in first place in their category.

I have grown both *S. nobilis* and *S. gigantea* and must admit that in bloom they look like something from another planet, which is their attraction for many people. Note that Stapelias, Hoodias and Huernias are difficult to grow and can be ungainly.

My first cactus candidates for a show would be some of the wonderful Epiphyllum hybrids, which have huge star-shaped flowers that are strikingly attractive. *Parodia aurespina* and the Rebutias (small plants) always gather crowds because the flowers are large for the plant and are so colorful (orange and golden yellow) that they look like silk flowers.

Mammillarias, somewhat large plants, produce fine flowers; *M. hahniana* and *M. reichenbachia* are worthy show candidates. *Echinocereus trichoglottis* with flashy and large orange-red flowers, is another good choice for entry. Many of the Echinopsis also have a good chance of catching a judge's eye; my *E. grusoni* (the golden ball), 12 inches in diameter, once won a ribbon. The small Lobivias bear fine large flowers; *L. famatimensis* and *L. hertrichiana* are worth entering in a show.

Remember that most cacti are on the endangered list, so buy only from dealers who propagate their own plants. Also, some of the species and varieties I recommend here might not be readily available; through garden magazine ads, exchange programs and plant society meetings (where members trade plants), there is a possibility of finding that elusive winning specimen. Here are more recommendations for cacti and succulents.

Cacti

Echinocactus horizonthalis
Echinocereus baileyii, E. dasycanthus
Echinopsis campylcantha, E. multiplex
Hylocereus undatus
Mammillaria bocasana, M. hahniana
Notocactus ottonis, N. scopa
Rebutia kupperiana, R. senilis
Zygocactus (many hybrids)

Succulents

Hawthorthia tesellata
Kalanchoe blossfeldiana, K. tomentosa
Stapelia variegata

GERANIUMS

The trailing ivy-leafed geraniums appeal to judges, and there are many varieties to grow. I especially favor 'Santa Paul', with its double lavender-purple flowers, and 'Charles Turner', with double pink flowers, for possible awards. 'L'Elegante' creates a basket of color and is tough for judges to ignore. For a big display, consider 'Estelle Doheney.' 'Comtesse de Grey', with single light pink flowers, and 'Mexican Beauty' are other worthwhile geraniums for exhibiting.

The Martha Washingtons (or Lady Washingtons) are regal plants for exhibition. They grow very large, and the two or three colors of the blossoms make them show stoppers. 'Lavender Grand Slam', with deep compact flowers, and 'Mood Indigo' are favorite winners. 'Black Lace', with maroon-edged flowers, and 'Santa Cruz' lead the way among the basket geraniums. The pansy geranium, 'Madame Layal', with purple flowers, brings rounds of applause from viewers. 'Carmen', 'Chorus Girl' and 'Easter Greetings' (with beautiful cerise flowers) are other good candidates for awards.

The fancy-leaved (zonal) geraniums are another good category to enter because the tricolors are brilliant and showy. 'Mrs. Henry Cox' is perhaps the best in this category, but I prefer 'Skies of Italy'. 'Pink Happy Thought' and 'Crystal Palace' are also notable. Among the silver-leaved varieties, 'Mountain of Snow' says it all.

There are so many excellent scented-leaved geraniums that it is hard to recommend just a few. I have always admired the large-leaved peppermint geranium, *Pelargo-*

nium tomentosum; the lemon-scented *P. crispum*, especially 'Prince Rupert' and 'Rollinson's Unique', which displays beautiful magenta flowers. Here are other excellent geraniums.

Ivy-Leaved

'Apricot Blossom'—salmon flowers

'La France'—semidouble lavender blooms

'Royal Blood'—semidouble flowers

Martha Washington

'Dubbonet'—ruffled wine-red flowers

'Gardener's Joy'—blush white flowers marked with
    rose

'Holiday'—ruffled white flowers touched with
    crimson

'Springtime'—rose-colored ruffled flowers

'African Belle'—pink flowers edged with maroon

'Georgia Peach'—large salmon flowers

'Voodoo'—maroon flowers

Fancy-Leaved (Zonal)

'Apple Blossom Rosebud'—white flowers edged in
  rose
'Better Times'—red flowers
'Dreams'—double salmon-pink blooms
'Fantasia'—semidouble red flowers
'Flare'—single salmon-pink flowers
'Harvest Moon'—single orange flowers
'Patricia Andrea'—brilliant rose-colored flowers
'Princess Fiat—double rose-pink blooms
'Painted Lady'—single red flowers
'Salmon Irene'—double flowers
'Red Rosebud'—double red flowers
'Snowball'—double white flowers
'Starlight'—single white blooms
'Summer Cloud'—double white flowers

Scented-Leaved

'Attar of Rose'—rose-scented blooms
'Lord Plymouth'—rose-colored flowers
'Dr. Livingston'—lemon-scented flowers
'Prince Rupert'—lemon-scented flowers
'Peppermint'—peppermint-scented blossoms

GESNERIADS

For years, the family Geseneriacae has been overshadowed by one member: Saintpaulia, the African violet. The other neglected members need notice, especially at flower shows. Frankly, I recommend skipping the African violet shows (there are so many) and concentrating on the other relatives.

I have always been fond of Aeschynanthus because of their fine red tubular-shaped flowers; these plants are handsome trailers. *A. pulcher* and *A. speciosus* are excellent in bloom, with long wands of red flowers that will make judges stop and stare. Even more awe-inspiring are the little-leaved Columneas, such as *C. arguta*, *C. banskii* and *C. microphylla*, with long trailing stems and multitudes of bright orange or red flowers.

The Episcias (peacock plants) have recently come into their own. Although somewhat difficult to cultivate, plants such as *E.* 'Acajou', *E. cupreata*, with handsome foliage and white flowers, and *E. dianthiflora*, with red flowers, deserve recognition. The variegated foliage and handsome flowers make these plants worthy of display at flower shows. Many new varieties are now available, so this category will become more important at shows as time goes by.

I have found that Kohlerias are very desirable houseplants. The Kohleria category is good to enter because not many people are cultivating the plants. *K. amabilis* is a fine basket plant with pink flowers; *K. erinthina*, with red flowers, is also impressive.

Rechstienerias and Smithianthas are fine plants yet not exhibited that often, so these are good categories to consider. *R. cardinalis* and *R. verticillata* are good species to grow. In the Smithiantha group, I especially like *S. cinnabrana*, with its orange-red flowers, and *S. zebrina*, with handsome foliage. Other good candidates include the following.

Aeschynanthus
A. lobbianus—brown tubular-shaped flowers

Columnea
C. arguta
C. 'Yellow Dragon'
C. 'Yellow Gold'

Episcia
E. 'Cameo'—handsome leaves and pretty red flowers
E. 'Emerald Queen'—red flowers
E. lilacina—fine lilac-colored flowers

Hypocyrta
H. strigillosa—orange flowers

Kohleria
K. 'Longwood'

Saintpaulia
Hundreds of worthy varieties

Streptocarpus
S. grandis—beautiful blue flowers
S. saxorum—large leaves and violet blooms

ORCHIDS

Of all the hundreds of plants I have grown, orchids are still my favorites. The information in this section pertains to my experience with shows in California, Illinois and Florida.

The Cattleya is the queen of the orchids. Yet this is the worst category to enter because you are competing against so many stunning plants. Enter only if you have a true specimen plant with numerous flowers.

Judges seem to always like the Lycastes; *L. skinneri* is a good candidate for a prize, with its large blush-white flowers and attractive appearance. Ascocentrums have now come into their own—*A. ampullaceum* and *A. miniatum* are excellent varieties to enter.

Well-grown Bifrenarias will almost certainly win you a prize. *Bifrenaria tryrianthina* is a stunner and grows well. Of all the hundreds of Dendrobiums, judges lean toward *D. chrysotoxum*, with its brilliant golden-yellow flowers in pendant scapes. Remember, however, that the flowers stay in good shape for only a few days. Judges also favor the stunning *D. densiflorum* and *D. thysriflorum*.

Epidendrums have always been the stepchild of the orchid world and so ignored by many growers, but not by judges. A good Epidendrum (or *E. encyclia*, as the plant is often called now), offers you a far better chance of winning an award than does a stellar Cattleya. Excellent Epidendrums (encyclia) for showing are *E. mariae, E. ciliare, E. prismatocarpon* and *E. radiatum* (the latter two always seem to win accolades).

Masdevallias, the cool-growing orchids from the Andes Mountains, look more like tiny kites than orchids and are always a sensation at flower shows. Good ones to cultivate are *M. spectabilis* and *M. coccinea* and its varieties.

Oncidiums and Pescatoreas are other good candidates for show entry. Usually *Coelogyne pandurata*, the famed black orchid from Burma, wins a prize. Avoid the overcrowded field of Vanda hybrids, such as the Ascocendas and other Vanda mixed breeds, because the competition is too fierce and the judges are very finicky in this category. Here are choice orchids to show:

Ascocentrum
A. ampullaceum—small plant, cerise flowers
A. miniatum—masses of brilliant orange flowers

Angraecum
A. leonis—dwarf, fine white flowers

Bifrenaria
B. harrisoniae—fine large white flowers
B. tyrianthina—large purple flowers

Coelogyne
C. massangeana—pendent scapes of brown flowers
C. pandurata—exotic greenish black flowers, yellow
     petals

Dendrobium
D. densiflorum—fine medium-size yellow flowers;
     pendent
D. superbum—long pendent stems filled with
     magenta flowers

Epidendrum (Encyclia)

E. radiatum—waxy white flowers, lined purple

E. mariae—beautiful white-and-green flowers

Laelia

L. anceps—large cerise flowers

L. tenebrosa—very large cerise-and-brown flowers

Odontoglossum

O. citrosum—frilled white flowers

O. ure skinneri—masses of purple flowers

Oncidium

O. ampliatum majus—tall scapes of brilliant yellow flowers

O. leuchochilum—many small yellow flowers

Pescatorea

P. cerina—brilliant waxy yellow flowers

Rhyncostylis

R. retusa—long scapes of small white-and-pink flowers

Zygopetalum

Z. mackayii—blue-and brown flowers; many varieties

CHAPTER THREE

How to Buy Plants

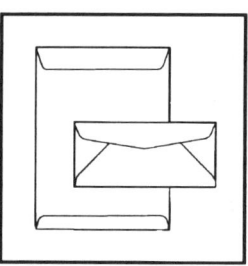

MAIL-ORDER COMPANIES

Mail-order house and trading among hobbyists are the best sources for many plants, such as begonias. Mail order is convenient: plants are described in the businesses' catalog, shipment is fast (usually only one week) and each species or cultivar is properly labeled and arrives in a peat or plastic starter pot. It is best to order plants in early spring or in the fall when the weather is fine for shipping and the plants have good weather in which to become established. In the summer, excessive heat can ruin a shipment, and winter shipment may be delayed because of awful weather conditions en route. Sometimes the mail-order supplier can supply mature plants; you will have to query the supplier before ordering. .

Mail-order companies (and there are many throughout the country) make their living from selling plants—generally in a specific category—begonias, orchids, bromeliads. These companies generally have reputable and devoted workers who care about plants, and you will get good plants when you order. Remember it is their sole business and, unlike florists shops, they do not have other avenues of profit such as wedding arrangements.

Most mail-order companies have catalogs, and some charge a fee while others do not. Some rebate the catalog fee on purchase of plants. Study the catalogs and order what you want. With today's methods of transportation, plants usually arrive in good shape. However, avoid having plants shipped in very hot or very cold weather.

There are various ways to have plants shipped—United Parcel Service, standard post office service and more (air is very expensive). I have found that standard priority mail from the post office is far better than most people think. There are, however, limitations on box size, so inquire first at your local post office.

See Appendix Three for a thorough listing of mail-order suppliers.

OTHER PLACES
TO BUY PLANTS

You can certainly buy plants at local nurseries, and occasionally you will come up with a find. I did when I came across a rare Hoya I had been seeking for a long time, but generally most nurseries only carry what is popular and what will sell readily, and they stay away from the odd or unusual plants (that are more likely to win at shows).

You can also trade plants with other hobbyists to secure a specific variety you want, and this can be done at plant meetings or by mail with other enthusiasts. When you trade among hobbyists, you have a chance of obtaining a species not usually available

Do not rule out finding a special plant at one of the giant stores such as K-Mart, Wal-Mart or Home Depot. Occasionally, you can pick up a really good plant and a bargain. Because these operations are so vast, and because the ordering for many stores is done at one place, the buyer really never sees the product—the plants are simply shipped to the stores. Quite often, a very rare plant will be included, so you have an opportunity to find a plant usually very hard to locate. I have made purchases of Cycads and Hoyas at local big markets where I never expected to find such plants. So keep alert.

Many people say they get good buys on plants at flea markets, and they probably do, but I have never really found anything worthwhile at the markets. Usually the plants are ordinary (but cheap).

At various shows usually held in shopping malls, you

can find some nice plants. There are orchid shows, bromeliad shows and other shows where plants are sold. Generally, the prices are quite high, but the plants seem to be in good shape (although do not expect to find anything exceptional). These companies that exhibit for sale at malls have a tendency to put plants for sale they themselves do not want. Rememeber that at award shows, you are up against these same collectors many times, so they rarely include anything of stellar value unless, of course, they are going out of business or simply need cash at that time.

Collectors have their own idiosyncrasies, and hanging on to rare or unusual species is frequent. So as far as I am concerned, certainly buy from these people, but be alert to the warnings given. Again I say that after three decades of plant buying, the mail-order supplier is your best bet.

CHAPTER FOUR

Where to House Your Plants

PLANT LOVERS WHO GROW A few houseplants have no
trouble locating their green treasures within their homes;
they grow their gems on a windowsill, on a table near a
window, hanging from a ceiling fixture in the living room
and elsewhere. But for those of you who are cultivating
prize-winning specimens, the growing area for your plants
is of utmost importance. You can devote a spare room to
your plants, use a plastic greenhouse or consider a solarium. As long as the growing area is convenient and
devoted solely to your specimen plants, you should have
no trouble maintaining your favored plants.

ROOM GREENHOUSES

Basically, a room greenhouse is an "envelope" for your plants, a clear plastic unit, generally 40 inches by 72 inches, that can be kept near a window. It sets up like a tent and is also available in a few other sizes. Some of the units have struts or other special devices to keep the structure rigid. These units are fine for a room devoted strictly to plants but not for display in other rooms in the home because they are not attractive. A room greenhouse is inexpensive, so it is something to consider in an out-of-the-way area. Be sure the greenhouse has adequate ventilation.

Another type of room greenhouse is custom-made of wood and looks like cabinetry. On a table or other display area it looks like a miniature palace. You can control the temperature, humidity and watering, allowing you low maintenance. However, these sophisticated units are expensive.

BEGONIAS

Tuberous begonias being grown for exhibition. Is there a winner in this group—perhaps for flower form and color. (photo by Matthew Barr)

This hirsute begonia is an unlikely candidate for a show win—the plant needs to be larger and more compact in growth. (photo by A. R. Addkinson)

Begonia mazae; the plant is too small and ill-formed to win any type of prize. Best to grow for pleasure on windowsill. (photo by Jack Kramer)

This angel-wing begonia similar to 'Lucerne' has good form, foliage color and heavy flowering. The top leaf should be trimmed to keep the compact, handsome growth pattern; a suitable container is also necessary. (photo by A. R. Addkinson)

BROMELIADS

In the Neoregelia group it is the foliage that makes the plant and this fine hybrid of Neoregelia concentrica *have good possibilities for a win; it is uniformly shaped and in flower. (photo by Bailey)*

The perfect flower spike of Vriesea carintata 'Rubin' makes this plant worthy of entry into a show. (photo by Jack Kramer)

A plain terra-cotta container would have been a better housing for Aechmea; the plant, how-ever, wins some points for the pendent floral spikes and fairly good growth habit. (photo by Jack Kramer)

An all-time favorite is Aechmea fasciata *with its star-shaped crowns of flowers and pink bracts. These plants often win at flower shows but competition is indeed stiff because of many new hybrids. (photo by Bill Shaban)*

GERANIUMS

One could surely find a winner in this group of fine Pelargoniums. (photo by Jerry Pavia)

Scented geraniums offer a great category at showtime. This Pelargonium, 'Concolor Lace', has an almost perfect "bouquet" of flowers and vivid color. (photo by Jerry Pavia)

This true geranium is Geranium incana, an old-time favorite, but not always a winner. (photo by Jerry Pavia)

GESNERIADS

Streptocarpus is a good category to enter in shows because not many people grow them—this species, S. saxorum, is quite handsome but shallow flower color and ill-formed flower bud in center ruins the possibilities. (photo by Bill Shaban)

The lipstick vine Aeschynanthus speciosus (lobbianus) always gets consideration at shows and this plant with fine flowers and good foliage has a chance to win an award. (photo by Bill Shaban)

The goldfish plant has created new interest in gesneriads and masquerades under two botanical names: Hypocyrta and Nematanthus. Full plants with an abundance of flowers and uniform canopy-type foliage growth would be prerequisites for a win—both lacking in this plant. (photo by Bill Shaban)

Don't enter this Gloxinia in a show—flowers are sparse and foliage has bad form. (photo by Jack Kramer)

CACTI AND SUCCULENTS

▼

This *Echeveria* hybrid has almost perfect form and the sculptural quality makes it a worthwhile plant. (photo by Bill Shaban)

In the *Mammillaria* group there are many species that stand out, and plants always have splendid flowers. Watch timing on show entries because flowers only last a few days. (photo by Bill Shaban)

Never overlook *Epiphyllum* varieties for a win at shows— there are so many hybrids in so many colors that the plants offer something for everyone. Again, be careful: these flowers only last a day or two so perfect timing is necessary for shows. (photo by Bill Shaban)

In the *Parodia* group there are many species that offer possible winners at shows because the plants bear large flowers for size of plants and most have brilliant color. (photo by Bill Shaban)

▲

ORCHIDS

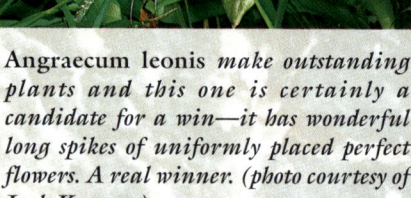

Angraecum leonis *make outstanding plants and this one is certainly a candidate for a win—it has wonderful long spikes of uniformly placed perfect flowers. A real winner. (photo courtesy of Jack Kramer)*

From the vast Dendrobium orchid family comes Dendrobium superbum var. alba—*a white fantasy of flowers on bare canes which makes quite a spectacle. Well-grown plants always get consideration at shows and some bloom with as many as one hundred flowers to a plant. (photo by Jack Kramer)*

This Epidendrum (Encyclia radiata) *is not an especially good plant for entry into a show but because these botanicals are seldom grown, even this example may have a chance for an award in its category. (photo by Jack Kramer)*

Always a showstopper is Ascocentrum miniatum. *With hundreds of small flowers, this plant is a winner in its category at almost any show. (photo by Jack Kramer)*

ORCHID WINNERS

Dendrobium aggregatum—*the profusion of flowers and perfect form makes this Dendrobium a good candidate for a ribbon. (photo by Jack Kramer)*

Lycaste skinneri—*a large flower, well formed and of large size puts this orchid in the running for an award. (photo by Jack Kramer)*

Ascocentrum ampullaeceum—*an orchid with fine color and not often shown, this plant could be a potential winner. (photo by Jack Kramer)*

Paphiopedilum praestens—*a rare and good candidate for a show. (photo by Jack Kramer)*

SHOW-STOPPERS

This wonderful red gloxinia could steal the show; wonderful flowers on a handsome plant. (photo courtesy of Jack Kramer)

Aechmea chantini 'Eldorado,' a stellar plant always demands attention at shows. This specimen has a good chance of a win. Note the uniform growth and perfect inflorescence. (photo by Jim Irwin)

The flowers of this Reiger begonia will steal the show—masses of them in bright color; foliage is healthy dark green—almost perfect. (photo courtesy of Jack Kramer)

This is a fine example of a prizewinning Pelargonium—the form is compact, the leaves in fine shape and the halo of flowers beautifully arranged by nature. (photo by Jerry Pavia)

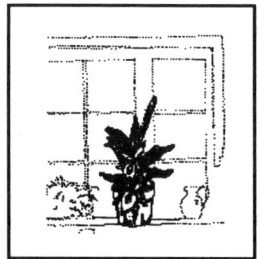

SPARE ROOM

A spare room (even a garage with adequate windows and a floor impervious to water) can be an ideal place for cultivating specimen plants. I once successfully raised superb cool-growing orchids in an unheated pantry in a Chicago flat. The advantage of a spare room is that you can customize it by installing redwood benches, putting in adequate fans for ventilation and adjusting the amount of light with curtains or shades. You can putter to your heart's content in your spare plant room without disturbing anyone else in the home and retreat to the room for privacy and escape from the chores of daily living.

Heating, cooling and ventilation are most important in the spare room. An eastern exposure is the best for plants because the light is not overly bright. A western exposure provides sunlight much too strong for most plants. For heating, extend your current heating system into the room, or install auxiliary heating facilities (these are similar to greenhouse heaters). Overhead fans are quite helpful for providing a welcome circulation of air.

SOLARIUMS

A true solarium is a tiled room with a drain and casement windows that provide sufficient light for growing almost any kind of plant, from an orchid to a begonia. These rooms were part of some houses built in the 1930s; my Chicago flat included a solarium, and I was able to cultivate my first prize-winning orchid, *Vanda caerulea*, the fabulous blue orchid. Conditions were ideal (even when the landlord turned off the heat at 11:00 each night). (Remember, most plants greatly benefit from a 10° to 15° drop in temperature at night.) If you really want to invest money into raising plants for show, you may want to consider having a spare room converted into a true solarium.

GREENHOUSES

A greenhouse is a great convenience, especially if you are growing dozens of plants. But a greenhouse can be tricky because it is of all-glass construction. It can become very hot in the summer and quite cold in the winter unless you install special heating and cooling devices. Also, in a greenhouse you must follow a strict regime of watering, plant protection, light control and other garden duties—I recommend you consult one of the many good books devoted solely to greenhouse growing.

CHAPTER FIVE

Protective Measures

IN CHAPTER SEVEN WE EXPLAIN the importance of packing plants for safe transportation to the flower show. Here we discuss another important protective measure: keeping insects off your plants. You do not want pests to dine on your favorite buds or flowers and ruin them before you can exhibit your entries.

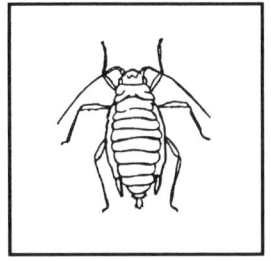

PESTS AND OTHER BUGS

If you grow plants, you will have to do some battle with insects. Ignore those advertisements claiming that certain chemicals will kill all the insects; with proper observation you can catch bugs before they take over and eliminate them by using simple nonpoisonous methods.

The bugs you have to watch out for are aphids, mealybugs, mites, scale, thrips, lace bugs and insidious ants. Yes, ants; they can destroy your plants without actually eating or boring into any part of the plants. Ants can cause more harm than a crop of mealy bugs because ants instinctively herd. And the insects they prefer to herd are mealybugs. The ants carry the mealybugs to plant parts where they keep the bugs so they have a food supply for future ants.

Unfortunately, ants do not respond to the simple remedies we recommend, so you will have to use ant traps. Several are available in supermarkets, home stores, hardware stores and in various other types of stores. I prefer the traps encased in metal because children and animals cannot get to the insecticide within the case. Set the traps in strategic locations.

FRIENDS AND ENEMIES

There are good bugs and bad bugs. Today you can buy good insects that will eat the bad ones. These insects do a fairly good job of eliminating any area of plant pests; consult the list of insectaries at the end of the book for places to buy "good" insects.

The nonpoisonous house spider is another friend in the plant area, eating various insects. I depend on chameleons here in Florida, which eat dozens of enemy insects; they defend my two-hundred plus plants quite successfully.

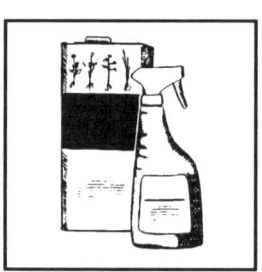

BOTANICAL REPELLENTS

Botanical repellents are insecticides made from various plants. They are not harmful and do not accumulate in the environment. These repellents include pyrethrum, a form of chrysanthemum; rotenone, a wood climber; Quassia, made from the crushed bark of a South American tree and hellebore, a member of the lily family.

Most of these organic repellents are sold at supply stores in powder or granule form. When you buy them, be sure to look at the contents indicated on the can or bottle to be doubly sure no insidious chemicals have been mixed with the natural product; many times such chemicals have indeed been added. Malathion, Diazinon and Benomyl are among the chemicals you do *not* want around your plants.

When using botanical repellents, follow instructions as prescribed, and always keep them on high shelves, away from children. Even though these are safe controls for plants, the repellents may be harmful if eaten.

OLD-FASHIONED REMEDIES

Sometimes the old ways are the best ways. Here are several old-fashioned pest preventatives I have been using for years.

Laundry Soap and Water

Detergents will not do; you must use laundry soap: 1/2 bar mixed *thoroughly* with 1 quart of water. Apply the solution with a cotton swab to the insect and to stems and leaf axils. Apply several times a day, at three-day intervals. This solution will eliminate mealybugs and aphids. You can also spray the solution on a plant. If you do, hose the plant with clean water after spraying the solution.

Rubbing Alcohol

Rubbing alcohol is a great eliminator of plant insects. With a cotton swab, douse the insect with the alcohol. This direct contact method works like a charm on mealybugs, aphids and other insects.

Nicotine and Water

Steep old cigarette tobacco in water for two days. Apply the solution with a cotton swab. Do *not* confuse this solution with nicotine sulphate, which is still sold in some places. Nicotine sulphate is much too toxic to work with.

Hosing

Take plants to a sink. With a strong stream of water, as with a sprayer attachment on the sink, dislodge and wash away insccts. This method is not as effective as the others, but it does work to some degree.

Pepper and Cinnamon

Many insects react badly to pepper or cinnamon. The condiments sold for food usage are fine; sprinkle them right on the bugs.

SECTION TWO

AT THE SHOW

CHAPTER SIX

Flower Shows

AMERICA WELCOMES SPRING WITH A multitude of really big and magnificent national flower shows where growers trot out their best plants and landscape ideas. Besides these events, year-round local flower shows sponsored by plant societies; exhibits held at county and state fairs; neighborhood, county and state garden club events and various other floral programs are held for flower aficionados' pleasure.

Winning is very ego-satisfying, no more so than at flower shows where experts in your avocation judge your horticultural ability. Chances of winning at a flower show are excellent because there are so many shows and so many categories to enter. Winning also spurs a gardener on to bigger things, and that flowering blue ribbon winner will be quite a conversation piece.

Innumerable flower shows are held throughout the country: national flower shows, regional shows, plant-society shows, arboretum shows, park shows and more. This book emphasizes the local shows that plant societies, such as the Orchid Society and the Cacti and Succulent Society, hold.

NATIONAL SHOWS

The larger flower shows have been held in the bigger cities for so many years that they are now traditions, such as the spectacular flower show sponsored by the Pennsylvania Horticultural Society in Philadelphia and the stellar New York Horticultural Society Flower Show. These floral events are held throughout the country, from Boston to Los Angeles. These shows present large displays of flowers, usually in landscapes, and attract thousands of visitors. Each show charges admission; the shows are attended by mail-order companies, landscape architects, designers, contractors and gardeners, among other plant lovers. Each show has a different theme each year; shows are publicized in newspapers, garden magazine and some general-interest magazines. You will enjoy the national flower shows, but be aware that they are mainly for viewing, not entering; their intent is to acquaint viewers with the thousands of flowers available.

Some flower shows such as those staged in Chicago, Boston, Philadelphia and other cities are large, almost mammoth, and you can spend a full day viewing presentations. These are mainly flower shows to excite and educate the public. A show might be local or a specific plant-society show and may include a single flower or many landscaped gardens. Single-flower shows are numerous as orchid and bromeliad enthusiasts are frequently showing. There are also several gesneriad and African violet single-flower shows.

The local show can be held in almost any type of building, from an exhibition hall to a bank to a country club or mall or lecture hall or even in a library. And there are also county shows (fairs) in which a flower show is part of the program.

In all of these events, awards are made for private individuals, commercial enterprises, nurseries and others. The awards depend on the show and what has been established and range from trophies to ribbons or cups.

These shows are highly publicized, and if you can attend, they are worth your time. The displays are spectacular, and dates and themes change yearly. If you are not an avid reader of garden magazines, your best bet is to write to the addresses listed in Appendix Four for further information.

PLANT SOCIETIES

The various plant societies have become, in the last decade, large organizations for hobbyist information and assistance. I strongly urge any garden enthusiast to join one of the societies (or more) of your favorite plant. There are reams of up-to-date information that societies provide that cannot be found elsewhere.

In addition to being able to attend plant-society meetings, you will also receive, with membership, the society's periodical, *The American Orchid Society Bulletin* for orchids, the *Bromeliad Bulletin* for bromeliads and so on. These publications are filled with wonderful information, and some have colored photos and information on reliable current places to buy your favorite plants.

Most societies have plant sales periodically where you can buy rare and special plants, and many offer raffles and other plant give-a-ways that are certainly worthwhile.

The yearly fee is really quite small for the amount of data that comes your way when you are a member of a plant society, and again I urge you to join. It is well worth the money (which in most cases may be deductible from your income tax).

Plant-Society Shows

In addition to the big national shows, there are hundreds of various other flower shows staged by local chapters of plant societies such as the American Orchid Society, the American Rock Garden Society and the African Violet Society of America, whose roster numbers more than thirty-five thousand members. During these local shows—which are held in almost every city, large and small—members exchange information about their favorite plants, sell plants, trade plants and compare notes on their horticultural failures and successes. Members also arrange vacation trips to the lands their favorite plants come from. Best of all, besides supplying wonderful camaraderie, plant societies make it possible for members to form new friendships, a definite plus today when meeting people in general is so chancy.

Certain plant societies also hold national shows (these shows are different from the national flower shows just discussed). For example, the Bromeliad Society holds a show each year in a different city, and the National Convention of the Begonia Society was held in Miami in 1993. If you are a member of a specific plant society, you will be notified of when and where the society will be holding both its local and national shows.

Appendix Two offers a listing of the horticultural societies for the more popular plants. Also indicated is whether the society has a bulletin and the names of the publications of the societies.

CHAPTER SEVEN

Showtime Basics

WHEN IT COMES TIME TO show your plants, there are certain duties to perform to be sure you are showing your plants to the best advantage. Cleaning containers, keeping plants symmetrical, labeling and obviously, maintaining the conditions of the flowers and buds must be considered. It makes little sense to exhibit plants that are not as perfect as possible in every respect.

Other basic considerations, sometimes forgotten in the rush, involve how you transport the plants the show. If you just pack plants in your vehicle helter-skelter, they will arrive in bad shape when you take them out of the vehicle because plants in pots have a tendency to fall over in driving time. So make suitable preparations and have boxes and other devices on hand to keep plants upright. It is always best to also have easy access to the plants—a standard automobile is not a good way to transport plants—a van (if you can get one) is better because it has back or side ingress and egress.

Also remember, it will take time to set up plants—if you are only entering one specimen you need not worry about it too much, but if you are entering several plants or are in a specific scene category, more time will have to be allotted to your setup. Rules of the show dictate just how much time you will have, so have everything needed on hand.

CONTAINERS

A clean terra-cotta pot is acceptable as a container unless the show schedule indicates a planter, a dish or any other different kind of container. Never, never cover the pot with foil or any decoration that detracts from your plant; remember, both the plant and its container are judged.

Salt deposits or algae frequently accumulate on clay pots, so clean the containers with a kitchen pot scrubber and hot water. Be sure the container is in proportion to the plant: a large plant in a small pot will get demerits, and a small plant in a larger container is downright unattractive. As a general rule, the plant (from the soil line) should be twice as tall as its container—this achieves good balance. Exceptions include low-growing rosette-type plants such as African violets, which look best in containers that are three-quarters as high as the diameter of the pot.

Plastic containers are acceptable at the flower shows. Be sure the container is clean and preferably dark green or black rather than a bright red or yellow. Be sure too that the container can take the weight of the plant because plastic pots tend to topple over.

BUDS AND FLOWERS

At flower shows, among the criteria plants are judged on are flower size, number of flowers to a plant and orientation of the flowers. The flowers must be of good substance, and no faded or dead flowers should be present. When you remove a dead or faded flower, also remove its stem, or the stem will cost you points when the plant is judged.

Flowers should look symmetrical with no crowded stems that make the plant look unbalanced. Pinch back lateral shoots because leggy and branching plants are unacceptable. Make sure the flowers are not one-sided (on only one side of the plant); flowers should be uniform in appearance.

Never enter a plant that is all bud. Some buds are fine, but judges look for plants with flowers, the majority of which are fresh and open.

TIMING BLOOMS FOR SHOWS

It is vitally important that your plants flower at the time the shows you want to enter are being held. First, be familiar with the bloom times of your species; you can gain this knowledge by experience, reading mail-order plant catalogs and various reference books, talking to other hobbyists and reading this book. When you find out the dates of the shows you are interested in, start preparing and grooming the appropriate plants. You can retard or accelerate blooming by lengthening or shortening days with artificial light and blackout curtains.

FOLIAGE

Besides looking for prime flowers on a plant, judges consider the plant's foliage and whether it meets certain standards. Foliage must be clean and balanced and in proportion to the flowers. Clean all leaves with a damp cloth, not a leaf-shining product. If stems are crowded with too many leaves, deftly remove some so the overall appearance of the plant is symmetrical. Again, keep foliage and flowers in proportion.

TRANSPORTING PLANTS TO THE SHOW

Getting plants to a show is not easy; if not done correctly, you can waste all your efforts. First, use a vehicle that is roomy enough to hold the plants, such as a station wagon or van. Next, be sure you have some trays or racks in which you can put plants upright and in which the plants will stay that way during travel time. Plants must be erect and protected from falling.

Expensive commercial plant racks are sold at wholesale florist suppliers. Less expensive are racks made from wood; make them yourself or hire someone to make them. With a coping saw, cut holes into baseboard; 3/4-inch plywood is fine. Holes should be large enough to accommodate the bases of the pots.

Carrying-cartons can also be fashioned from one-gallon plastic bottles, plastic milk cartons or cottage cheese containers. Place the cartons in a large box, and wedge paper between each container to prevent them from tipping over. Or crumple tissue paper on top of the soil, and then tape across the paper to the sides of the pot to keep the soil from falling out. I also form wads of newspaper into a rope and wrap each rope around each pot, taping the ends of the rope together. This thick rope is a protective girdle that prevents each pot from breaking or cracking if your vehicle hits a bump or the container is dislodged.

To protect buds and flowers during transport, place cotton over them and then wrap the cotton with tissue. Do not put rubber bands or string around the tissue; just twist the tissue and it should stay in place. When you unwrap the tissue, gently pull the cotton away from the bud or flower. I prefer the cotton and tissue to the excelsior many hobbyists use.

Begonias, orchids and tender plants must be in a well-heated vehicle; even a bit of cold can damage these plants. Finally, be aware of what you are doing when you open the vehicle to load or unload plants. Many of my flowering stems were nipped by the top of my van as I bent over to put the carrying cases into the van.

SETTING UP
YOUR EXHIBIT

The actual setup or arrangement of your plants at the flower show is of prime importance. You can avoid chaos and being frenzied by knowing beforehand where the staging is to be, how the exhibits are to be arranged, how you can safely unload and reload your plants and exactly how much space you have been allotted.

Just where you will be in the show depends on the various divisions and classes you have entered. Do not be upset if your assigned space is, say, a back area or a less predominant area because judges make thorough inspections; whether you are in front or in the back, you should get a fair judgment. If you are showing at a local show, you will have about three or four hours to set up your exhibit. At large shows, more space is available, so more chaos is involved as all the competitors set up. Generally, each exhibitor's space is denoted by a card with the exhibitor's name on it; the card is placed face downward.

It is important that all labels are legibly printed and that plant names are spelled correctly. (Points are deducted for misspelled names). Place your label directly in front of the plant where it clearly defines which plant the label is for. Do not put the label in back of or to the side of the plant.

CHAPTER EIGHT

Judging

THE PEOPLE WHO JUDGE PLANTS are more than qualified and include wholesale growers and plant experts. The judges (usually three) know a good plant when they see it, and they will take considerable time to make their decisions, which is done in a closed session.

Flower-show judges must meet very rigid standards. Judges pass through a sort of apprenticeship: student judge for 3 years, probationary judge, accredited judge and, finally, senior judge.

Judges must be well versed in such categories as color perception and form of flower, pass training programs, attend seminars and be thoroughly familiar with all the rules and regulations of the shows.

POINT SCALES

Each category of plants—whether the plant is a begonia or an orchid—has a point scale, with one hundred points being perfection. The breakdown of the general point scale is this:

1. Form of flower   30 points
2. Color of flower   30 points
3. Other characteristics   40 points
    a. Size of flower (10 points)
    b. Substance texture (10 points)
    c. Arrangement of inflorescence (10 points)
    d. Floriferousness (10 points)

As an example, here is the point system for Cattleya orchids, as outlined in the *American Orchid Society Handbook on Judging and Exhibition.*

1. Form of flower   30 points
    a. General form (15 points)
    b. Sepals (5 points)
    c. Petals (5 points)
    d. Labellum (5 points)

2. Color of flower   30 points
    a. General color (15 points)
    b. Sepals and petals (7 points)
    c. Labellum (8 points)

3. Other characteristics   40 points
    a. Size of flowers (10 points)
    b. Substance and texture (20 points)
    c. Floriferousness and stem (10 points)

Such a point system is generally applicable throughout the various genera.

    See Appendix One for other point scales.

AWARD-WINNING PLANTS

Various types of awards are given; within the orchid shows, such awards include Certificates of Cultural Merit (CCM) and Certificates of Horticultural Merit (CHM) among others. There are numerous trophies, ribbons, cash or certificates for classes of plants. You can win First Place, Second Place, Third Place, Best of Show or Honorable Mention. Your chances of winning an award are excellent if you enter the right class with your best plants properly labeled with the correct name(s).

    Each flower category—African violets, cacti and succulents, bromeliads, for example—has different rules. Your plants should be labeled correctly, have near-perfect flowers (remove all dead or faded leaves or flowers) and be planted in clean containers. The plant is what is being judged. This means the entire plant, from the bottom of the pot to the top of the leaves. Even the appearance of the container is considered: it should be clean and in the proper proportion to the plant.

The plant is judged by its general appearance; overall aesthetics are quite important. Is the plant growing properly, that is, straight, twining or whatever is indicative of that plant? Are leaves free of blemishes, spots and insect marks? Are the flowers in proportion to the size of the plant? A large plant should be staked properly and standing in its container, not flopping over the sides. No dead roots, such as in orchids, or the faded leaves prevalent in begonias should be showing.

The plant must be labeled legibly with its current Latin botanical name (whether a species or a hybrid) spelled correctly on a tag neatly affixed to the plant. If you are not sure of the correct name of your plant, send a picture to a plant expert or to a college or person with authority in that field and ask for the proper identification. You can also check names in the various horticultural dictionaries, such as the *Royal Horticultural Society Dictionary of Plants* or in *Hortus III*. Be neat; a scrawled pencil notation on a piece of cardboard will count against you.

See Chapter 7 to learn more details about entering shows and all that is involved. You will also find out some interesting cultural facts about orchids, begonias and other favorite flowering plants.

CHAPTER NINE

After the Show and Onward

YOU HAVE SHOWN YOUR PLANTS and, whether the plants have won or not (remember there is always next year), treated them kindly when you get them back home. Plants that have been exposed to a different environment for several days, that have been transported back and forth, have gone through a somewhat traumatic experience—out of their natural surroundings—air, temperature, humidity and light. There are some things you can do to make the conversion less stressful to the plant.

RECONDITIONING

When you put your plant back into the growing area, do not immediately water the soil. Allow the plant to rest—dry out for a few days before you begin your regular care regime. Try to position the plant where it was before you took it to the show. Many plants have the peculiar habit of not responding to care once they have been moved—even an inch one way or the other can make a difference, so try to replace the show performer(s) where they were originally.

After a few weeks of appropriate care—watering and feeding (this can start again after a month), make some decision about the plant and its possibilities next year as a candidate for a show. Perhaps it just isn't up to the standards of the show (you will know this now), perhaps there were too many candidates in the same category and it might be better to concentrate on other varieties.

Make some judgments now about which plants to enter in the next show, and collect and grow with those goals in mind.

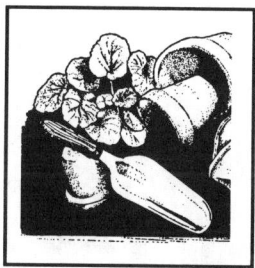

FILLING THE VOID

If at the show you noticed only a few candidates in a particular category, this may be the area to try and win a ribbon next year. There are generally fewer entries in one category than others—keep your eyes open and hopefully you made some notes so you can make a good choice.

Do not be afraid to enter rare species—your chances of winning are tenfold if you and only one other exhibitor have the only entries. If the show was crowded with lovely hanging begonias (and they usually are), avoid this category.

Obviously, if you select a category of specific species and that plant is rare and hard to find, you will have to do some hunting, but you have time now and it is fun to try to find odd species or varieties to show. There are several ways you can locate new plants, and the mail-order route is what you take (see Chapter 3).

Rules and Regulations

THE FOLLOWING DATA IS GENERAL but gives sufficient information on how various groups of plants are exhibited in classes (categories) and some rules of various shows. Obviously, rules sometimes change, but generally show format and particulars remain the same.

Of the six groups of plants in this book, I have included data on Begonias, Bromeliads, Geraniums, Gesneriads and Orchids. (I omitted Cacti and Succulents because of space limitations and redundancy.)

GENERAL RULES AND REGULATIONS

Entry regulations for shows—orchids, begonias, bromeliads and others vary slightly, but most shows include the following general rules:

All entries must be registered by the entry clerk.
You must enter proper plant in proper classification.
All plants must be correctly labeled.
Labels must be prominantly displayed.

All entries must remian in place for duration of show.

Judges have the right to award or withhold any scheduled trophy or ribbon.

No duplicate awards given.

All entries exhibited must have been grown for at least
six months.

The judges may use only the point system (scoring) as
approved by each specific society.

Judge's decisions are final.

BEGONIAS

Whether a local show from a chapter or a national yearly
show, there are many classes of begonias—and the class in
which you enter a plant depends upon the items discussed
in this book. In general, begonias are judged much the same
as orchids, bromeliads or others—by the point system.
And as in the other plant shows, there are many categories:

Cane-like
Under 2 feet
Two to 4 feet
Over 4 feet
Shrub-like
Hairy-leaved
Thick-stemmed
Trunk-like
Semperflorens
Rhizomatous
Crested or spiral rhizomatous
Rex
Tuberous
Species

Each category is further broken down. For example, Cane-like is further broken down into subcategories according to size, leaf color and other qualities. You can secure flower show booklets, pamphlets, from your local society chapter.

BROMELIADS

These plants have gained popularity in the last decade and even include special shows for a specific genus as in the case of Tillandsias. Generally, most bromeliad shows have the following classes or categories:

Specimen single stem plants
Specimen multiple stem plants
Multiple plants
Potted
Mounted
Blooming
Foliage

Point system is usually (but not always) as follows:

Foliage plants	Merit Judging	Major Awards
Cultural perfection	30	25
Conformation	30	30
Color and marking	30	30
Difficulty of cultivation		10
Maturity of plant	10	5

GERANIUMS

Geranium shows are scheduled throughout the country at various times. The general rules and organizational structure are about the same as for all flower shows: class, size of flowers, flower color and foliage. The classes are usually as follows:

Pelargonium (Lady Washington types)
Ivy-leaved
Fancy-leaved
Scented-leaved
Dwarf
Others

This classification can vary. Standards, Hanging Baskets and Espalier are often other classes; each show defines its own specialties.

The point scale ranges from 90 to 100 for first place, 85 or over for second place, and 75 or over for third place. An honorable mention is generally awarded as well.

The condition of the plant accounts for 30 to 40 points. The size, form and number of flowers earn 10 (or more) points, depending on the division. Flower color is worth 10 to 20 points, and foliage earns 10 to 20 points. Here is a simplified scale of points for judging geraniums:

Pelargonium hortorum

Condition of plant	30 points
Size and form of flowers	20 points
Flower color	20 points
Flower substance	20 points
Foliage	10 points

Fancy-Leaved

Condition of plant	30 points
Size of flower	5 points
Flower color	5 points
Flower substance	10 points
Foliage	50 points

Ivy-Leaved (*Pelargonium pelatatum*)

Condition of plant	30 points
Size and form of flowers	20 points
Flower color	15 points
Flower substance	15 points
Foliage	20 points

Scented-Leaved

Condition of plant	30 points
Size of flowers	10 points
Flower color	10 points
Flower substance	5 points
Foliage	45 points

AFRICAN VIOLETS
(INCLUDING OTHER GESNERIADS)

The African violet is a favorite plant, and shows are held throughout the country—your plant society will keep you posted. The general rules are complicated, so you need to write to your society for information. Generally, there are categories for all types of African violets:

Standard plants—single and semidouble blossoms
Standard plants—double blossoms
Standard plants—single, semidouble or double blossoms
Miniature plants
Trailers and species
Specimen plants
New cultivars
Specimen African violets

These classifications can vary with other specialties included.

The point scale applies here as for other shows—namely, points for condition of plant, number of flowers, flower color, foliage and other qualities.

SCALE OF POINTS FOR JUDGING GESNERIADS (OTHER THAN AFRICAN VIOLETS)

Sinningia; Rechstieneria

Form	25 points
Quality of bloom, buds	15 points
Quantity of bloom	25 points
Color of bloom	10 points
Condition	25 points

Gesneriads Grown Primarily for Bloom

Culture	20 points
Quality of bloom	15 points
Quantity of bloom	25 points
Condition	20 points
Size	10 points
Color	10 points

Gesneriads Grown Primarily for Foliage

Culture	40 points
Condition	25 points
Distinction	10 points
Size	10 points
Ornamental value	15 points

New Cultivars

Culture	20 points
Floriferousness	15 points
Condition	15 points
Desirability of plant	10 points
Distinction	10 points
Rarity	15 points
Labeling	15 points

ORCHIDS

There are so many orchid shows—local and regional—it is hard to keep track of what is going on where. The American Orchid Society Bulletin does a fine job of listing shows monthly in their excellent bulletin.

Current American Orchid Society scale of points for judging varies for artistic arrangements, for specific plants and so forth.

Here are the classes for general show awards:

Species—bifoliate, unifoliate
Cattleya hybrids—white
Cattleya hybrids—white colored lip
Cattleya hybrids, orange yellow, bronze, etc.

Cattleya hybrids—lavender

Brassocattleya (Bc and Blc)—various colors: white, colored lip, lavender, pink   art shades—bronze, orange

Epidendrum species—Encyclia types

Epidendrum hybrids

Intergenerics—Epidendrum or Encyclia and other genera

Phalaenopsis species—colors (all hybrids):white, yellow, pink; stripes, spots, bars

Phalaenopsis intergeneric hybrids other than Doritaenopsis

Best Phalaenopsis flower

Doritis

Doritaenopsis (same schedule as Pahalensopsis)

Vanda species (strap leaf)

Vanda species and hybrids (terete)

Vanda hybrid (strap)—yellow

Vanda hybrid (strap)—red

Vanda hybrid (strap)—blue

Vanda hybrid (semiterete)

Rhynchostylis, species or hybrid

Renanthera, species or hybrids

Asocenda, species or hybrid

Asocenda, flower under 2 inches

Asocenda, flower over 2 inches

Other species

Other hybrids

Dendrobiums

Dendrobiums, phaalaenopsis type

Dendrobium, pendulous type

Dendrobium, nobile type

Dendrobium, antelope type

Dendrobium, cane section—aggregatum, chrysotoxum
Dendrobium other than above

Oncidium and Allied Genera

Equitant, species or hybrid
Species, other than equitant
Hybrid, other than equitant
Miltonia species or hybrids with Miltonia

Slippers (Paphiopedilum)

Species
Hybrid
Best Slipper

Horticultural Societies and Garden Organizations

American Horticultural Society
Joseph Keyser
7931 E. Boulevard Drive
Alexandria, VA 22308
(703) 768-5700
The American Horticulturist (six issues a year)

California Horticultural Society
Mrs. M. Mueller
1847 34th Avenue
San Francisco, CA 94122
(415) 566-5222
Pacific Horticulture Magazine (four issues a year)

Horticultural Society of New York
Angela Guierrez
128 W. 58th Street
New York, NY 10019
(212) 757-0915
HSNY Newsletter (four issues a year)

Massachusetts Horticultural Society
300 Massachusetts Avenue
Boston, MA 02115
(617) 536-9280

Indoor Gardening Society of America
530 S.W. Hamilton Street
Portland, OR 97221
(503) 292-9785
Indoor Garden (six issues a year)

National Gardening Association
Member Subscription Service
Depot Square
Peterborough, NH 03458
(802) 863-1308
National Gardening (twelve issues a year)

The Pennsylvania Horticultural Society
Elizabeth Gullan
325 Walnut Street
Philadelphia, PA 19106
(215) 625-8250
Green Scene (six issues a year); *PHS News* (eleven issues a year)

Plant Amnesty
Cass Turnbull
906 N.W. 87th Street
Seattle, WA 98117
Newsletter (six issues a year)

The Royal Horticultural Society
Membership Secretary
80 Vincent Square
London, England SW1P 2PE
The Garden (twelve issues a year)

Where to Buy Plants

MAIL-ORDER SUPPLIERS

The following is by no means a complete list of mail-order companies that sell plants. And the omission of your favorite company is not intentional. The companies I list are the ones I have personally dealt with for years and feel confident in recommending for specialty plants:

Begonias and Geraniums

Logees Greenhouses
141 North Street
Danielson, CT 06239

For years a fine source of begonias of all kinds—hundreds of varieties. Highly recommended. Catalog charge $3 refunded with order.

Kartuz Greenhouse
1408 Sunset Drive
Vista, CA 92083

Always a reliable source.
Write for catalog.

Merry Gardens
P.O. Box 595
Camden, ME 04843

Another good supplier; always ships fine plants. Write for catalog.

Tinari Greenhouse
P.O. Box 190
2325 Valley Road
Huntington Valley, PA
19006

Fine variety of begonias; other plants as well. Write for catalog or list.

Bromeliads

Alberts and Merkle
Federal Highway
Boynton Beach, FL 33435

Fine assortment of bromeliads. Catalog charge.

Oak Hill Gardens
P.O. Box 25
Route 2 Binnie Road
Dundee, IL 60118

Excellent stock; many kinds of bromeliads. Catalog free.

Seaborn Del Dios Nursery
P.O. Box 455
Route 3
Escondido, CA 92025

Primary bromeliad source. Color catalog free.

Shelldance Nursery
2000 Cabrillo Highway
Pacifica, CA 91044

A broad selection of bromeliads. Catalog charge.

Corneilson Bromeliads
225 San Bernadino
N. Fort Meyers, FL 33903

List only; write for details.

Holladay Jungle
P.O. Box 5727E
Fresno, CA 93755

Tillandsias; retail list available

Cacti and Succulents

Henriettas Nursery
1345 N. Browley Avenue
Fresno, CA 93722

Good selection of both cacti and succulents. Catalog charge.

Grigsby Cactus Gardens
2354 Bella Vista Drive
Vista, CA 92084

Write for catalog.

Orchids

Oakhill Gardens
P.O. Box 25
Binnie Road
Dundee, IL 60618

Large selection of orchids; species and hybrids. Catalog free.

Rod McLellan
1450 El Camino Real
S. San Francisco, CA 94080

Good selection of orchids, many hybrids. No catalog. List only

Orchids by Hausermann
2N 134 Addison Road
Villa Park, IL 60181

Wide choice of many orchids; all sizes all kinds. Catalog charge.

Orchid World International   Good selection of orchids.
10885 S.W. 95th Street
Miami, FL 33176

RF Orchids   Specialist in Vandas and allied
28100 S.W. 182nd Avenue   genera. Catalog free.
Homestead, FL 33030

Carter and Holmes   Unusual species. Catalog
No. 1 Old Mendenhall Road   charge.
P.O. Box 668
Newberry, SC 29108

Gesneriads

Buell's Greenhouses   Big variety of gesneriads.
P.O. Box 218   Catalog list charge.
Weeks Road
Eastford, CT 06242

Coda Greenhouses   Wide choice of gesneriads.
P.O. Box 8417   Catalog charge.
Fredericksburg, VA 22404

Lee Violettes Natalia   Good choice of gesneriads.
P.O. Box 206   Catalog charge.
Beecher Falls, VT 05902

Lyndon Lyons Greenhouses   Fine choice of geseneriads.
14 Multchler Street   Catalog charge.
Dolgeville, NY 13329

Tiki Nursery   Wide variety of gesneriads.
P.O. Box 187   Catalog charge.
Fairview, NC 28730

Plant Shows

SUBJECTS AND THEMES FOR EACH flower show change from year to year. Please call for updated information.

ANN ARBOR

March

ANNUAL ANN ARBOR
FLOWER AND GARDEN SHOW

This horticultural show features growers and landscape designers, plant society exhibitions and retail sales. The show is held at

Washtenaw Farm
Council Grounds
5055 Ann Arbor-Saline Road
Saline, MI 48176

For further information, contact

Matthaei Botanical Gardens
Attn: Margaret Vergith
1800 N. Dixboro Road
Ann Arbor, MI 48105
(313) 998-7061

ATLANTA
February

ATLANTA FLOWER SHOW

This sixth year of the exhibit features landscaped gardens, educational exhibits, free seminars and retail sales. It is sponsored by the Atlanta Botanical Garden and held at the

Atlanta Apparel Mart/INFORUM
240 Peachtree Street
Atlanta, GA 30303
(404) 876-5859

BOSTON
March

NEW ENGLAND FLOWER SHOW

Sponsored by the Massachusetts Horticultural Society, this exhibition has 4 acres of landscaped and designed gardens in bloom, plus exhibits and professional and amateur horticultural displays. The next show will be held at the

Bayside Exposition Center
200 Mt. Vernon
Boston, MA 02215

For information, contact the

Massachusetts Horticultural Society
300 Massachusetts Avenue
Boston, MA 02115
(617) 536-9280

CHARLOTTE, NORTH CAROLINA
February

SOUTHERN SPRING SHOW

This show will be held at the

Charlotte Merchandise Mart
2500 E. Independence Boulevard
Charlotte, NC 28236

For information, contact

Southern Shows, Inc.
P.O. Box 36859
810 Baxter Street
Charlotte, NC 28236
(704) 376-6594

CLEVELAND
February

50TH ANNIVERSARY CLEVELAND HOME AND FLOWER SHOW

This show displays landscaped competition gardens, two landscaped homes and horticultural displays. It is held at the

Cleveland Convention Center
Cleveland, OH 44114

For information, contact

Building Expositions, Inc.
113 St. Clair Avenue, N.E.
Suite 300
Cleveland, OH 44114
(216) 621-3145

DISTRICT OF COLUMBIA
March

WASHINGTON FLOWER AND GARDEN SHOW

The show includes more than 2 acres of gardens in full bloom and a large retail area. It is held at the

Washington Convention Center
900 Ninth Street at New York Avenue N.W.
Washington, DC 20001

For complete information, call (703) 569-7141.

LOS ANGELES
(RANCHO PALOS VERDES)
February

CHELSEA AMERICA FLOWER SHOW

This show is patterned after but not affiliated with the Chelsea Flower Show held annually in England by the Royal Horticultural Society. (A similar show is held later in the month in Palm Beach, Florida.) For complete information, contact the

Chelsea America Foundation
8854 Third Avenue
New York, NY 10022
(212) 207-1774
Fax (212) 750-9664
or call (310) 648-6602

MINNEAPOLIS
March

SPRING HOME AND GARDEN SHOW

Sponsored by the Minnesota State Horticultural Society, this regional show includes professional and amateur exhibits. It is held at the

Minneapolis Convention Center
3rd and Grant
Minneapolis, MN 55404

For information, call (800) 676-MSHS.

NEW ORLEANS
April

ANNUAL SPRING GARDEN SHOW

This garden show features displays by plant societies, garden centers, commercial suppliers and government agencies. It is held at

New Orleans Botanic Garden
City Park Avenue
New Orleans, LA 70119
For information, call (504) 486-3736 or (504) 482-1107.

NEW YORK
March

NEW YORK FLOWER SHOW

This mammoth show features educational horticultural and gardening displays and large floral and garden designs and is held at

Pier 92
W. 51st Street and 12th Avenue at the Hudson River
New York, NY 10020

For information, contact the

Horticultural Society of New York
128 W. 58th Street
New York, NY 10019
(212) 757-0915

PALM BEACH, FLORIDA
February

CHELSEA AMERICA FLOWER SHOW

This flower show, launched in 1993, is based on the Chelsea Flower Show held annually in England. It is held at the

Vista Center
Okeechobee Boulevard (West Palm Beach exit of Florida Turnpike)

For complete information, contact the

Chelsea America Foundation
885 Third Avenue
New York, NY 10022
(212) 207-1774
Fax (212) 750-9664
or call (407) 793-7577

PHILADELPHIA
March

PHILADELPHIA FLOWER SHOW

Our oldest flower show celebrates classic designs and perennial gardens. Besides the fifty landscapes by nurseries and horticultural organizations, seven hundred individual exhibitors compete at the

Philadelphia Civic Center
34th Street and Civic Center Boulevard
Philadelphia, PA 19104

For complete information, contact the

Pennsylvania Horticultural Society
325 Walnut Street
Philadelphia, PA 19106
(215) 625-8250
Fax (215) 625-8288

ST. LOUIS
January

ST. LOUIS FLOWER SHOW

This annual flower show, hosted by the Junior League of St. Louis, includes landscaped display gardens, floral displays, speakers, tours and three days and two nights at a local hotel, a lecture and luncheon and a tour of the Missouri Botanical Garden. The show is held at the

Cervantes Convention Center
801 Convention Plaza
St. Louis, MO 63131
(314) 997-3407

SAN FRANCISCO
April

SAN FRANCISCO LANDSCAPE GARDEN SHOW

This show, presented by the Friends of Recreation and Parks, is the major fund-raiser for Golden Gate Park and is held at

Fort Mason Center
Piers 2 and 3
San Francisco, CA 94105

For information, contact

Friends of Recreation and Parks
Janet Tabet-Coppola, Show Director
McLaren Lodge
Golden Gate Park
San Francisco, CA 94117
(415) 750-5108

SEATTLE

February

NORTHWEST FLOWER AND GARDEN SHOW

This show has thirty-eight demonstration gardens and major exhibits, classes, seminars and slide lectures featuring leading horticulturists. The show takes place at the

Washington State Convention and Trade Center
8th and Pike Streets
Seattle, WA 98101

For complete information, contact

Northwest Flowers and Garden Show
1515 N.W. 51st Street
Seattle, WA 98107
(206) 789-5333

Plant Societies

African Violet Society of American, Inc.
P.O. Box 3609
Beaumont, TX 77704
(409) 839-4725
African Violet Magazine (six times a year)

American Begonia Society
John Ingles, Jr.
8922 Conway Drive
Riverside, CA 92503
(714) 687-3728
The Begonian (six issues a year)

American Bonsai Society
Anne D. Moyle
P.O. Box 358
Keene, NH 03431
(603) 352-9034
Bonsai Journal (four issues a year); *Abstracts* (three issues a year)

American Camellia Society
C. David Scheibert
P.O. Box 1217
Fort Valley, GA 31030-1217
(912) 967-2359
The Camellia Journal (four issues a year); *American Camellia Yearbook*

American Daffodil Society, Inc.
Mary Lou Gripshover
1686 Grey Fox Trails
Milford, OH 45150
(513) 248-9137
The Daffodil Journal (four issues a year)

American Dahlia Society
Michael Martinolich
159 Pine Street
New Hyde Park, NY 11040
Bulletin (four issues a year)

American Fuchsia Society
County Fair Building
9th Avenue at Lincoln Way
San Francisco, CA 94122
Bulletin (monthly)

American Gloxinia and Gesneriad Society, Inc.
Ellen Todd, Membership Secretary
P.O. Box 493
Beverly Farms, MA 01915
The Gloxinian (six issues a year)

American Hemerocallis Society
Elly Launius, Executive Secretary
1454 Rebel Drive
Jackson, MS 39211
(601) 366-4362
Daylily Journal (four issues a year)

American Hibiscus Society
Jeri Grantham, Executive Secretary
P.O. Box 321540
Cocoa Beach, FL 32932-1540
(407) 783-2576
The Seed Pod (four issues a year)

American Orchid Society
Victoria Robb Creech
6000 S. Olive Avenue
West Palm Beach, FL 33405
(407) 585-8666
Bulletin (monthly); *AOS Awards Quarterly*

Bromeliad Society, Inc.
2488 E. 49th Street
Tulsa, OK 74105
Journal (six issues a year)

Cactus and Succulent Society of America
Louise Lippold
P.O. Box 3010
Santa Barbara, CA 93130
Cactus & Succulent Journal; *CSSA Newsletter* (six issues a
year each)

The Cycad Society
David Mayo
1161 Phyllis Court
Mountain View, CA 94040
(415) 964-7898
The Cycad Newsletter (four issues a year)

Epiphyllum Society of America
Betty Berg
P.O. Box 1395
Monrovia, CA 91017
(818) 447-9688
The Bulletin (six issues a year)

Gardenia Society of America
Lyman Duncan
P.O. Box 879
Atwater, CA 95301
(209) 383-4251
Gardenia Quarterly

Gesneriad Society International
2119 Pile Street
Clovis, NM 88101-3597
Gesneriad Journal

Index